THE

INTENTIONAL

FAMILY

Also by William J. Doherty

*Soul Searching: Why Psychotherapy Must
Promote Moral Responsibility*

Medical Family Therapy

Families and Health

Family Therapy and Family Medicine

THE

INTENTIONAL

FAMILY
How to Build
Family Ties
in Our Modern World

William J. Doherty, Ph.D.

ADDISON-WESLEY PUBLISHING COMPANY, INC.
Reading, Massachusetts • Menlo Park, California • New York
Don Mills, Ontario • Harlow, England • Amsterdam • Bonn
Sydney • Singapore • Tokyo • Madrid • San Juan
Paris • Seoul • Milan • Mexico City • Taipei

Part of Chapter Eight appeared in the *Family Therapy Networker* and is reprinted with permission.

Excerpts from Sylvia Kaplan's manuscript, "Ritual and Ceremony as a Major Life Development Resource for Healing and Bind up the Wounds of Divorce," are printed with permission.

Many of the designations used by manufacturers and sellers to distinguish their products are claimed as trademarks. Where those designations appear in this book and Addison-Wesley was aware of a trademark claim, the designations have been printed in initial capital letters.

Library of Congress Cataloging-in-Publication Data

Doherty, William J. (William Joseph), 1945–
    The intentional family : how to build family ties in our modern
 world / William J. Doherty.
        p.   cm.
    Includes bibliographical references and index.
    ISBN 0-201-69466-2 (alk. paper)
    1. Family—United States.   2. Family festivals—United States.
 3. Rites and ceremonies—United States.   I. Title.
 HQ536.D64   1997
 306.85´0973—dc21   96–40283
                                                              CIP

Jacket design by Suzanne Heiser
Text design by Dede Cummings
Set in 11-point New Aster by A&B Typesetters, Inc.

1 2 3 4 5 6 7 8 9-MA-0100999897
First printing, June 1997

For Leah, Eric, and Elizabeth

Contents

Part IV
BECOMING A MORE INTENTIONAL FAMILY

Acknowledgments

THIS BOOK WAS 15 YEARS IN GESTATION, starting with a talk I gave in 1981 on the topic of families at the holiday season. Once I began to pay close attention to holiday rituals and then to other kinds of family rituals, a new vista on family life opened up to me. It took another decade, however, before I saw the connection between families' rituals and their ability to survive and prosper in our contemporary world. I began to see how being "intentional" about family life through family rituals was the best antidote to the drift of contemporary family life toward less closeness, less meaning, and less community. The world is not a friendly place for families these days, and those who lack a plan for their survival and growth are apt to be casualties.

Over the past 15 years my own family has grown more intentional about our life together and especially about our family rituals. I have written about these experiences in this book because they have been so important to my thinking about families in general. I have also learned from the many hundreds of families I have worked with as a marriage and family therapist over the past 20 years, and from the families who have participated in my talks and workshops. Their stories, altered to protect privacy, are told in this book. My children Eric (age 23) and Elizabeth (age 21) not only have been my teachers about family life but also gracious in allowing me to share their stories with a wider public.

I am grateful to Patrick Dougherty, Elizabeth Horst, Sally Maison, and Ann O'Grady-Schneider for their careful reading and thoughtful comments on an earlier draft of the book, and to my agent Jim Levine for keeping hope alive that I would find an outlet for these ideas. My editor, Liz Maguire, has been a cheerleader and thoughtful adviser during this process. Special thanks to my friends Peter Skipper and Sylvia Kaplan and their families for being willing to share their stories and use their names.

I wrote the bulk of this book during a retreat at Two Harbors, Minnesota. Every day I went to Louise's Coffee Shop to drink coffee and think about the next chapter. What I found there was a center of community in that small town. I saw how Louise created a space for a wide range of people, some healthy and some disabled, to ritualize their friendships and ties to their neighbors. Being there helped to inspire my writing.

Finally, I am grateful to my wife Leah who has been so close to this book and its ideas since their origins, and who has consistently believed I had something important to say. She was my first reader and reliable critic for each chapter; if an idea or a piece of writing didn't fly with Leah, I grounded it. During the writing, we celebrated our twenty-fifth wedding anniversary with full hearts and with wonder about the passing of the years. How could I write a book about family life without Leah's presence on every page?

The Intentional Family

Part I

THE

INTENTIONAL

FAMILY

CHAPTER

ONE

The Intentional Family

W<small>E REINVENTED FAMILY LIFE</small> in the twentieth century but never wrote a user's manual. Have no doubt about the reinvention. This century has witnessed a revolution in the structures and expectations of family life. The changes in family structures are by now familiar: A child is as likely to grow up in a single-parent family or stepfamily as in a first-married family; an adult is likely to cohabitate, marry, divorce, and remarry; and most mothers are in the paid labor force.

The revolution in expectations of family life is less widely recognized. A scene from the 1971 film *Lovers and Other Strangers* captures this cultural shift. Richie, the adult son of Italian immigrant parents, tells them that he and his wife are divorcing. The stunned parents want to know "What's the story, Richie?" When he tells them he is not "happy," the answer does not compute. "Happy?" the father retorts, "What? Do you think your mother and I are happy?" A startled Richie asks, "You mean you and Mom aren't happy?" The parents look at each other, shrug, and with one voice respond, "No. We're content." Richie storms off with the testimonial of his generation: "Well, if I'm not going to be happy, I'm not going to stay married." But the memorable line from this vignette comes from the mother, played by Beatrice Arthur: "Don't look for happiness, Richie; it'll only make you miserable."

These fictional immigrant parents represented the remnants of the Institutional Family, the traditional family based on kinship, children, community ties, economics, and the father's authority. For the Institutional Family, the primary goals for family life were stability and security; happiness was secondary. Ending a marriage because you were not "happy" made no sense. An elderly British lord expressed the values of the Institutional Family when, upon learning that I was a family therapist he commented: "A frightful mistake so many people are making these days [is] throwing away a perfectly good marriage simply because they fall in love with somebody else."

The Institutional Family was suited to a world of family farms, small family businesses, and tight communities bound together by a common religion. The dominant form of family life for many centuries, it began to give way during the Industrial Revolution of the nineteenth century, when individual freedom and the pursuit of personal happiness and achievement began to be more important than kinship obligations, and when small farms and villages started to give way to more impersonal cities. During the 1920s, American sociologists began noting how an historically new kind of family—what I term the Psychological Family—was replacing the Institutional Family of the past. This new kind of family was based on personal achievement and happiness more than on family obligations and tight community bonds. In the early twentieth century, Americans turned a corner in family life, never to go back.[1]

By the 1950s, the Psychological Family had largely replaced the Institutional Family as the cultural norm in America. In ideal form, the Psychological Family was a nuclear unit headed by a stable married couple with close emotional ties, good communication, and an effective partnership in rearing children in a nurturing atmosphere. The chief goals of this kind of family life were no longer stability and security. Instead, the overarching goal was the satisfaction of individual family members. Men's and women's roles ideally were "separate but equal," with men being experts on the "world" and women being experts on the home.

Current social debates about the Traditional Family generally center around this Psychological Family, which did not come into full flower until the 1950s. Its supporters praise its traditional values, while its critics decry its conformity and unequal gender roles. Both sides miss an important point: the Psychological

Family was radical in its own right when it supplanted the Institutional Family as the dominant family form. Its emergence threatened historical family values by reversing the importance of the individual and the family. The family's main job now was to promote the happiness and achievement of individual family members, rather than individual family members' main job being to promote the well-being of the family unit. To paraphrase: Ask not what you can do for your family; ask what your family can do for you. No more radical idea ever entered family life, but it is one we now take for granted in mainstream American culture.

If you doubt this shift in family values, try to imagine a contemporary American man choosing a wife because his family thinks the match would be good for the family. Or imagine a young woman announcing that she will never marry in order to stay home to care for her aging parents. Or a young adult deciding not to have sex before marriage in order not to bring embarrassment to his or her family. Most of us would assume that there was much more to these stories; someone was not telling the truth, or there was some personal or family pathology at work. We would have trouble imagining that a healthy adult would sacrifice important personal goals for the sake of family duties. Although most Americans continue to assume that parents, especially mothers, should place family needs over personal needs while the children are being raised, all bets are off for young people's obligations to their parents and extended family. And the perceived absence of happiness in marriage is a widely acceptable reason to divorce and try again for the kind of satisfying intimate relationship that has become a cultural birthright.

From its beginning, the Psychological Family was germinating the seeds of its own destruction. It harbored a profound contradiction: the value of individual happiness for both men and women, coupled with the value of family stability. For marriage, this meant commitment based on getting one's personal needs met in an equal relationship—a dicey combination for couples that lacked the skills required for such unions. When the feminist and sexual revolutions exploded in the late 1960s and later joined with the "Me Generation" of the 1970s, the Psychological Family began to fracture. The power of high expectations for marriage overwhelmed couples' abilities to cope at a time when divorce was losing its social stigma. The divorce rate skyrocketed along with nonmarital births and single-parent and stepfamilies. The cultural image of the two-parent nuclear family from cradle to grave splintered into a montage of family forms.

The eclipse of the shared cultural ideal of the Psychological Family gave rise to the Pluralistic Family, which has dominated the last three decades of the twentieth century. Unlike the Institutional and Psychological Families, the Pluralistic Family does not offer an ideal for what constitutes a good family. Instead, the working assumption is that people create, or find themselves in, a wide variety of family configurations. No family form is inherently better than another, and all should be supported by the broader society. The traditional two-parent family becomes one lifestyle alternative among others, including cohabitation, single parenting, remarriage, and gay and lesbian families. The Pluralistic Family ideal is to let a thousand family forms bloom as families creatively respond to the modern world.

The Pluralistic Family carries forward the Psychological Family's emphasis on personal satisfaction but adds the new value of *flexibility:* to be a successful sailor in the seas of contemporary family life requires the ability to shift with the winds that come your way and the willingness to change boats when necessary. Essentially, you can never tell which kind of family structure you or your children may end up in, so be flexible.[2]

> We now have the first society in human history without a clear social consensus about what constitutes a "real" family and "good" family. And I don't see one emerging anytime soon.

There is intense debate over the merits of the Pluralistic Family ideal in contemporary society. These cultural debates reflect a struggle between adherents to the Psychological Family and the Pluralistic Family. (Hardly anyone wants to go back to the Institutional Family because the value of personal satisfaction in family life ranks high among virtually all groups in American society, with the exception of recent immigrants.) But the very existence of the cultural debate shows the strength of the idea of the Pluralistic Family: the two-parent Psychological Family competes as just one lifestyle ideal among others. We now have the first society in human history without a clear social consensus about what constitutes a "real" family and "good" family. And I don't see one emerging anytime soon.

Following these staggering twentieth-century changes in family life, we now live in the best and worst of times for families. The worst of times because families have historically followed the guidance of their community and culture in shaping marriage, childrearing, and the countless other elements of family living; and now the community and culture are unable to provide a coherent vision or set of tools and supports. Families are left to struggle on their own. We also live in the best of times because we understand better what makes families work, and because now we have unprecedented freedom to shape the kind of family life we want, to be *intentional* about our families.

DEFINING THE INTENTIONAL FAMILY

Sometimes with my therapy clients, I use an analogy of the Mississippi River, which flows just a couple of miles from my office. I say that family life is like putting a canoe into that great body of water. If you enter the water at St. Paul and don't do anything, you will head south toward New Orleans. If you want to go north, or even stay at St. Paul, you have to work hard and have a plan. In the same

> The natural drift of family life in contemporary America is toward slowly diminishing connection, meaning, and community.

way, if you get married or have a child without a working plan for your family's journey, you will likely head "south" toward less closeness, less meaning, and less joy over time. A family, like a canoe, must be steered or paddled, or it won't take you where you want to go.

The natural drift of family life in contemporary America is toward slowly diminishing connection, meaning, and community. You don't have to be a "dysfunctional" couple to feel more distant as the years go by, or a particularly inept parent to feel that you spend more time disciplining your children than enjoying them. You are not unusual if you feel you have too little time for meaningful involvement with your community. Lacking cultural support and tools for shaping the kinds of families we want, most of us end up hoping the river currents carry us to somewhere we want to go. In the "anything goes" world of the Pluralistic Family, where specifically do we want to go, and how in the world do we get there?

> Only an Intentional Family has a fighting chance to maintain and increase its sense of connection, meaning, and community over the years.

Only an Intentional Family has a fighting chance to maintain and increase its sense of connection, meaning, and community over the years. An Intentional Family is one whose members create a working plan for maintaining and building family ties, and then implement the plan as best they can. An Intentional Family rows and steers its boat rather than being moved only by the winds and the current.

At heart, the Intentional Family is a ritualizing family. It creates patterns of connecting through everyday family rituals, seasonal celebrations, special occasions, and community involvement. An Intentional Family does not let mealtimes deteriorate into television watching. It does not let adolescents "do their own thing" at the expense of all family outings. It is willing to look at how it handles Christmas or bar mitzvahs in order to make them work better for everyone. It has the discipline to stick with good rituals, and the flexibility to change them when they are not working anymore.

The Entropic Family

The opposite of the Intentional Family is the Entropic Family. Entropy is the term for the tendency of a physical system to lose energy and coherence over time, such as a gas that expands and dissipates until there is little trace left. Similarly, the Entropic Family, through lack of conscious attention to its inner life and community ties, gradually loses a sense of cohesion over the years. Its maintenance rituals such as meals and birthdays lose their spark, and then degenerate. Individual family members may have active lives in the world, but the energy of the family itself slowly seeps away.

Contemporary society creates Entropic Families by two means. First is our lack of support for couples to make marriage work and for parents to make childrearing work. We generate the highest expectations of family life of any generation in human history, but provide the least guidance as to how to achieve success in our contemporary family forms. We struggle as a society over the most basic kinds of family support, such as unpaid leave for caring for babies and sick family members. And we have barely begun to face our joint responsibility to help families learn the skills for parenting, partnership, and intimacy that most of us expect of family life. No wonder that the odds of a happy lifetime marriage are probably no more than one in four—half of new couples divorce and another quarter are probably not very happy.

The second way that we collectively create Entropic Families is by putting up barriers to sustaining family rituals. Cars, televisions, busy work schedules, consumerism, and a host of other forces propel family members along fast-moving, diverging tracks. Family meals become casualties of soccer practice, violin lessons, work demands, and the lure of a favorite television rerun. Tired parents lack energy to focus the family on reconnecting at the end of the workday. The Christmas holidays appear before family plans are in place, and vacations are patched together at the last minute.

In Entropic Families, there is no less love, no less desire for meaning and connection than in Intentional Families. But their members gradually drift apart because they lack the infusions of bonding, intimacy, and community that only well-maintained family rituals can give. In the end, most families that are not intentional will follow the currents of entropy toward less closeness than they had hoped for when they started their family journey; the forces pulling on families are just too strong in the modern world. Ultimately, we must decide either to steer or go where the river takes us. The key to successful steering is to be intentional about our family rituals.

FAMILY RITUALS

When you recall your favorite memories of childhood, probably they center around family rituals such as bedtime, an annual vacation, Thanksgiving, Christmas, or the weekly Sabbath meal. Your worst memories might also be connected with these family rituals. Interestingly, many family researchers and family therapists have learned only recently how significant a component family rituals are to the glue that holds families together.[3] Previously, most researchers and therapists emphasized *talk:* how couples communicate, how parents verbally praise and discipline children. But as important as talking is, what professionals weren't considering was how we *enact* our family relationships.

Family rituals are repeated and coordinated activities that have significance for the family.[4] To be a ritual, the activity has to have *meaning* or *significance;* otherwise, it is a routine but not a ritual. For example, most families' bathroom activities are routines rather than rituals because they do not have much symbolic importance, although such an activity can become a ritual. For example, one of my clients and his new wife took a shower together every morning, which became a ritual for them. To be a ritual, then, the activity must also be *repeated*; an occasional, unplanned trip to a cabin would not make for a family ritual, whereas an annual trip that family members look forward to would. Finally, a ritual activity must be *coordinated*; a meal that each person fixes and eats alone would not qualify as a family

ritual, whereas a meal that everyone gathers deliberately together to eat would, if done regularly and with meaning.

A goal of this book is to show you how to transform some family routines into family rituals. Family rituals give us four important things:

Predictability. The sense of regularity and order that families
require, especially those with children. Knowing that the
father will talk to his child and read a story every night
makes bedtime something to look forward to and savor. If
bedtime talks and stories have to be negotiated every night—
if there is no predictability—then the ritual loses its power.

Connection. The bedtime ritual may be the primary one-to-
one time shared between a father and his child. For couples, bedtime rituals may also be an important opportunity
to connect emotionally and perhaps sexually after a busy,
distracted day. Couples who value rituals of connection generally make sure they coordinate their evening plans so as
to go to bed together. Those who generally go to bed at different times are apt to lose connection over time, unless
they have strong alternative rituals of connection.

Identity. A sense of who belongs to the family and what is special about the family. You may know who your core family
members are by who is invited to the Thanksgiving meal;
including nonrelatives in core family rituals makes them
"family," too. Families who take interesting vacations together acquire the self-image of a fun-loving family. They
will say "We are campers" or "We are hikers." For some couples, shopping for antiques becomes a ritual outing that
helps form a couple identity as antique lovers.

A way to enact values. Values demonstrate what we believe and
hold dear. Religious rituals are a good example, as is a family volunteering together for community work; or ensuring
that the children join in regular family visits to a grand-
parent in a nursing home, thereby teaching that it is important to honor and support this elderly family member.[5]

Types of Family Rituals

Family rituals by definition involve more than one family member, but not all family rituals necessarily involve the whole family. Some rituals involve just two members; say, a married couple going out to dinner or a parent reading to a child. Some involve subgroups, as when my father took my sister and me to Philadelphia Phillies baseball games. Some involve the larger extended family, such as family reunions and holiday rituals. Others include close friends of the family, and still others, a larger community such as a church or synagogue or a volunteer group to support the local children's museum. It is important to think of the different combinations of participants in family rituals. Successful Intentional Families learn to ritualize everything from pairs to communities.[6]

I like to classify family rituals by the *function* they play for families; that is, by the needs they serve. Thus, there are rituals for connection or bonding, rituals for showing love to individual family members, and rituals that bind the family to the larger community.

Connection rituals offer everyday opportunities for family bonding, such as family meals, morning and bedtime routines, and the comings and goings of family members to and from work and school. They also involve family outings, from small trips to the ice cream store to major family vacations. The goal is a sense of family bonding.

Love rituals focus on developing one-to-one intimacy and making individual family members feel special. They can be subdivided into couple rituals and special-person rituals. Examples of couple love rituals are anniversaries, Valentine's Day, "dating," and sexual relations. Special-person rituals generally center around birthdays, Mother's Day, and Father's Day.

Community rituals have a more public dimension than connection and love rituals. They include major family events such as weddings and funerals that link families to their communities, as well as religious activities in churches, synagogues, or mosques. In addition, community rituals include conscious efforts to connect with a wider social network than the family, to both give and gain support. Too much writing about family life has ignored the public face of families and concentrated narrowly on the internal hearth and home. The healthiest families give to their communities and receive support back in good measure.

Thanksgiving and Christmas have evolved into a special category of family ritual, involving all three functions of rituals: connection, love, and community. They are the grand rituals of the calendar year for the majority of American families, Christian and non-Christian alike. And for many people, holiday rituals hold both the fondest and most depressing memories of childhood.

Historians have learned recently that community rituals, not "home" rituals, formed the linchpin of family life in the era of the Institutional Family. Before the mid-nineteenth century in Europe and America, family rituals hardly existed as we know of them today. Ritual activities occurred mostly in community settings such as churches and public commons, not inside the family itself. Families had daily routines, of course, but apparently they did not regard them as significant sources of family connection. They ate meals, but they did not think of family dinners as a special time separate from other times. Indeed, families prior to the late nineteenth century did not dwell much on their interior life. Christmas was celebrated with community festivals, not with family rituals of celebration and gift-giving. Families did not have birthday parties, and couples did not celebrate anniversaries. It was only with the passing of the Institutional Family and the gradual emergence of the Psychological Family after the Industrial Revolution that families began to think of themselves as separate from their communities and in need of special family rituals. As their urban environment grew more alien and as fathers went into the workforce away from home, families began to cultivate their inner world through special rituals. When communities broke up, families had to become intentional about their own rituals.[7]

There is no universal yardstick for measuring family rituals for all of our diverse contemporary families. Remarried families have different needs from first-married families, as do single-parent families from two-parent families. Different ethnic traditions require different degrees of flexibility or structure in family rituals. Some families are tied closely to their ethnic origins and to their extended families, and some have more independent lifestyles. Some families have young children, some have adolescents, and some have no children. Some families are experiencing peaceful periods in their life, and thus feel free to be creative with their rituals, while others are undergoing tremendous stress and need to just hang on to what they have. There is no ritual formula that applies to all this diversity. Indeed, the idea of the Intentional Family is encourage families to use their own values, histories, religions, and cultures to consciously plan their life together and in community.

TAMING TIME AND TECHNOLOGY

Becoming a ritualizing Intentional Family means learning to manage the two principal drains on the energy of most American families: time demands outside the home and electronic technology inside the home.

Now that most mothers are employed, and fathers are working as much or more than ever, there is a net decrease in the amount of time parents have to spend with their children and with each other. Add to that the fact that jobs for teenagers are plentiful, and many of them are also employed during family dinner hours and on weekends. And middle-class families in particular now spend a huge amount of time driving their children to various lessons and practices, on top of attending their games and events. If time is the raw material of family rituals, we are suffering from its shortage. Many American families feel starved for time.[8]

How can we become more intentional about family life in the face of this time shortage? Let's say you are already an overwhelmed single parent, or a married person who barely has time to talk to your spouse. Will thinking about enhancing your family rituals just serve to make you feel even more guilty than you already do? Two general strategies will be exemplified throughout this book. First is to make better use of the time you already spend on family activities. You have to feed your children, so start with improving the quality of those feeding rituals, without lengthening the time. You have to put your kids to bed; work on making it more pleasurable. You probably have birthday parties, holiday celebrations, and countless other family activities. You can enhance their quality while not adding to their number or extending their time requirements.

Disconnecting the Wires

The second general strategy is to experiment with carving out time from another activity that occupies more than its fair share of your attention. I recommend taming technology. We live in an era of the wired American family. The average American family has 2.5 television sets, and the average American spends over four hours per day watching television. That means television watching consumes half of our nonsleep, nonwork time. You can't tell me there is no surplus family ritual time to be carved out there! Add in CD players, telephones, and, increasingly, computers and the Internet. When we are in our cars, there is the radio and tape player. When we are out for walks, there are head phones. When we are running errands, more of us talk on cellular phones. We are always interruptible and distractible, two conditions that work against family rituals and intentional family life.[9]

Believe me, I am not a Luddite, rejecting all modern technology. When my daughter was in Europe, the telephone and e-mail kept us in contact. And television watching can be a relaxing way for family members to unwind. But, for many of us, electronic technology is the pet that has taken over the house. That's the bad news. The good news is that taming it even a little, such as by turning off the television during meals, can free up time for family rituals. We trained our dog to stay out of our bedrooms, and we banned television from there as well. No one, including the dog, has suffered for it.

The idea behind the Intentional Family is that families can decide for themselves, based on their own traditions, values, and circumstances, how best to ritualize their lives. Most families have some rituals they enjoy, some they don't enjoy but feel stuck with, and some they could benefit from creating or refurbishing. As you read this book, I encourage you to develop an agenda of current rituals you might want to remodel and new ones you might want to try. But hold off on trying anything new on your family until you read the last chapter, where I discuss specific strategies for creating and modifying family rituals. Moving too quickly or unilaterally in the domain of family rituals is sure to result in your family members saying "No way!" to your creative ideas. Changing family rituals requires sensitivity, tact, timing, and diplomatic skills—the very talents necessary to survive as an Intentional Family in an era of both unprecedented confusion and opportunity for families.

Part II

FAMILY

RITUALS

OF

CONNECTION

CHAPTER

TWO

Family Meals

THE HOVLANDS GAVE UP ON FAMILY DINNERS years ago. Nobody can remember why. Perhaps it was when their twin girls, Ashley and Rebecca, reached the age at which they started to insist on eating what they wanted when they wanted. Perhaps it was when the father, David, started coming home later from his job. Perhaps it was when the mother, Ruth, went back to work as a nurse and came home tired at the end of every day. Whatever the reasons, the Hovlands don't do dinner as a family anymore. They don't do breakfast or lunch either, for that matter.

So what's the damage to this family? The Hovlands share strong bonds of affection; the parents get along well; and the daughters, now age 16, have normal adolescent problems amplified somewhat by sibling conflicts between twins. The family has enough income to keep major economic worries at bay, and they have good friends and good-enough relations with their extended families. They are living the American dream, in some ways. It's just that they lack a focus to their family life, a sense of being a group, of having a center to their common life—except for once a year when they traditionally vacation together at a cabin in northern Minnesota.

The Hovlands are an underritualized family, as the following typical dinner scenario illustrates. Sometime between 5:30 and 6:30 P.M., one of the girls wanders into the kitchen and asks Mother what's for dinner. Ruth reports on the options, usually food in quantities for one or two people, but not four. Over the years, Ruth, who is solely in charge of meal planning and shopping, has opted for simple dishes that family members can microwave or prepare solo at the stove. That might mean a couple of pieces of chicken, a frozen pizza, hamburger left over from a picnic with friends, a box of macaroni and cheese, minute rice, hot dogs, a couple of frozen dinners, and fixings for a salad. The all-American teenager's menu, except for the salad.

Ashley or Rebecca—whoever shows up first—picks through the options in the refrigerator, makes a selection, and either asks Mom to prepare it or does so herself. She eats at the kitchen counter on a stool and looks at the comics in the paper or the television in the background. Ruth hovers around the kitchen and, on and off, engages in conversation with her daughter. Ruth may then start getting her own dinner together, or call to her other daughter to inquire what she wants. At most, two family members will be eating at the same time—and quickly. By the time David comes home around 6:30, generally everyone else has eaten. Ruth has prepared him something that he eats hurriedly while going through the mail. Sometimes, Ruth holds off her own meal until David comes home and the two eat at the kitchen table instead of the counter, but even then the television is on, and David may start reading the paper.

The Hovland family accomplishes the biological function of family meals: they ingest food. But they come up short on the social function of family meals—to bond and connect as family members. This perhaps would not be a problem if they ritualized other aspects of their family life, but other than their annual vacation, they are "ritual minimalists." The result is a surface quality to their interpersonal connections, an undertone of taking one another for granted, and a subtle behavior of entitlement in the children—as in "I expect my immediate needs to take precedence over family activities." Although the Hovlands care for one another and are supportive to one another in crises—as when Ashley thought she was pregnant last year—having regular family dinners together requires an everyday, disciplined allegiance to the common family good, which the Hovlands lack. The forces of entropy pull them apart more strongly than the forces of connection bind them together.

The D'Antonio family is in many ways the opposite of the Hovlands. The parents, Al and Linda, are second-generation Italian-Americans with a strong sense of family obligations. Family dinners are a must. In their family traditions, even after adult children leave home, they are expected to return for Sunday dinner. Their three children are two daughters, ages 5 and 8, and a son, age 15. Family dinners start precisely at 6:00 P.M., which is now a problem because 15-year-old Joey works at Burger King after school on weekdays and doesn't get off work until 6:00 P.M. No accommodation is made for his job; instead, his parents complain that his job is interfering with family dinner and that he should ask his boss to change the schedule.

Everyone at the D'Antonio table is expected to eat—and finish—all the food served. And because the children's food preferences are sometimes at odds with their parents', there are frequent conflicts over how much the children are eating and whether they will earn dessert. These family dinners are often the only time the parents and children are together during the day, so the parents, especially the father, also use the time to inquire about the children's schoolwork and friends, freely interjecting comments and criticisms.

Not surprisingly, the D'Antonio children have decidedly mixed feelings about their family dinners. When the atmosphere is positive, the meals are a source of family bonding as well as good food. When the atmosphere is negative, as it often is, the children dread dinners. The parents, for their part, see meals as a family duty, but approach them with too much rigidity and season them with too much instruction and too many demands. In their hearts, they don't enjoy family meals either. Thus, families like the D'Antonios, who try to cling to family meals but with too much rigidity and conflict, often devolve into the next kind of family.

The Moores still have family dinners, but as a hollow ritual. Half the time they graze separately like the Hovlands; and the other half, they eat dinner while watching television. Sally Moore, now a single parent, remembers the days when she and her ex-husband were continually scolding the children about their eating habits, when their two boys yelled and fought at table, and when she and her husband argued over how hard to be on the boys. At some point, the parents gave up the struggle to have family conversations during dinner. This was not a conscious decision, however. One August the family got into the habit of watching the Olympics on television during dinner, and they never turned the set off. Focusing on the television instead of one another lowered the tension level at dinner. Family members came and went from the table as they pleased, and the only arguments were over which show to watch. Now when the children are with their father on weekends, they either go out for fast food or eat in front of the television at his home.

These three families had different approaches to a common problem: how to maintain family dinner rituals. The Hovlands gave up family meals entirely. The D'Antonios held on rigidly to a style of family meals that was not working for them. The Moores alternated between skipping family dinners and escaping via the television.

These are not atypical American families. A 1995 national survey found that less than a third of American families eat dinner together most nights, a figure down substantially from the 1970s. Most adults say that they had more family dinners during their childhood than they do now in their own homes. When they do sit down together to dinner, over half of American families say they have the TV on. But when asked, the great majority of people say they believe that family dinner is one of the most important ways to maintain family communication; and most believe that regular family dinners contribute to children's success in school. If families value dinner rituals so highly, why do they have them less frequently than they would like? Conflicting schedules is by far the number one reason given, followed by being rushed, work, and school activities.[1]

Not only do contemporary families have difficulty finding time for dinner, even when they do eat together, family arguments are common. Researchers who have observed family dinners have noted the frequency of conflict, especially with children, regarding eating and table manners.[2] When most of us start a family, we fantasize that dinnertime will be one of bonding and warm conversation. But this does not happen automatically. Without an intentional approach, family meals can become a dull routine or even a source of significant disenchantment.

One Intentional Family's Dinner Ritual

The Robinsons wouldn't recommend to other families that they do family dinners in this way, but the following ritual has worked well for them since the children, now late adolescents, were toddlers.

They try to start dinner about the same time every night, allowing for flexibility when they know in advance that someone will be late. This start time, generally 6:00 P.M., has served them well as the children became adolescents and were out and about in the community after school.

When the children were preschoolers, the Robinsons began lighting two candles during dinner (during the Christmas season, they light an Advent candle). The children, Ben and Nicole, took turns blowing out the candles, and now that they are older, they light the candles on most days. Then their father, Joe, lowers the dimmer switch on the dining room lights as the family sits down to eat. The effect of the candles and the dimmed lighting is to quiet everyone's senses and prepare them for time together. The conversations are generally relaxed and low-key.

The family stays at the table until everyone is finished and one of the parents signals that they can leave. Since the mother, Cathy, generally prepares the meal, the father and children clean up. Now that the children are older, they both set the table and clean up on their own.

Although there are no set topics for family dinner conversation, and no banned emotions, Cathy and Joe have learned over the years to avoid problem-oriented talk during dinner. This is not the time to inquire about why last night's homework was not done, or why the children were fighting after school that day. After years of trial and a lot of error, the parents also stopped hassling the children about their eating habits. Instead they instituted a dinner rule that the children had to try everything served to them, but could decline to finish something they did not like. The parents would sometimes coax the children to continue eating their food, but did so without anger and without threats to withhold dessert. By the time the children were teens, even these food discussions had ceased. For their part, the children were expected to be respectful to the cook if they did not like a dish. They could say they did not like something, but were not allowed to disdainfully declare that the food was terrible.

Settling on these procedures for family dinners took a number of years, but they worked well for the Robinsons. No family is perfect, of course, and no family ritual unblemished, including the Robinsons. Sometimes Cathy feels burdened by being the main meal planner and executor; Joe prepares just one meal per week. Sometimes Joe tends to rush through the meal if he has work to do in the evening. And as the children get older and have jobs and afterschool activities, it has become more difficult to have full family meals every night. Nevertheless, the Robinsons feel proud of how they have used their family dinners to provide a base for emotional connection over the years. Being intentional about this everyday ritual has solidified their family. When they are having their family dinners regularly, they feel more connected during the rest of day and evening, and there are fewer irritable arguments and attention-seeking conflicts.

FAMILY RITUAL PHASES

Just as a fine meal has more than one course, family rituals have more than one phase; in fact, there are three: a transition phase, an enactment phase, and an exit phase.[3] Paying attention to these discrete stages of family rituals can help you to troubleshoot what is not working in your current rituals and figure out where to strengthen them.

The Transition Phase

The transition phase is used to move from everyday matters into "ritual space," where the sense of ceremony and connection are enhanced. Think of a Sunday religious service at a church. People generally first enter a public gathering area, where conversations may occur at everyday voice levels. Then they enter the sanctuary itself, where conversations are held in hushed tones or not at all. The final element of the transition to the religious ritual begins when the organist starts the first hymn.

In family rituals such as dinners, the transition phase is crucial. The Hovland family has no coordinated transition to the dinner meal; everyone starts meals on their own. Likewise, when the Moores make television part of their transition, they limit their ability to focus on either eating or family connections. The D'Antonios do set the table and begin eating at the same time, which gives them a basic transition into the meal ritual, but it is too rigid to be comforting. Only the Robinsons pay careful attention to their transition to family dinners. After the food is placed on the table, they light candles and lower the dining room lights. The father then closes the door between the dining area and the cluttered kitchen area. This gesture establishes a physical boundary between the work in the kitchen and the ritual world of the dining room. The Robinsons also turn on music to create a mood for the family meal. They are highly intentional about arranging the physical environment for their family dinner ritual, which is no doubt why their meals are so satisfying. For religious families, a prayer can be a good way to mark the transition from everyday interaction to dinner interaction, and it connects the family to its wider religious community and belief system.

The Enactment Phase

The enactment phase is what is done during the ritual itself. At church, it is the actual ceremony. During family meals, it is the eating of food and interacting among family members. The purpose of the enactment phase is to give the family a sense of connection and mutual enjoyment. After all, eating is one of the most pleasurable of human activities, and eating with loved ones can enhance the pleasure significantly. The Hovlands don't have a coordinated family meal very often, and when they do, they focus on eating more than talking. The D'Antonios have clear patterns of eating and communication during meals, but too much conflict invades the ritual, thereby diminishing the sense of family connection. The Moores often enjoy one another as they watch a favorite television show together and talk intermittently during meals, but they don't sustain enough focus on the meal and their conversation to gain maximum benefit from the ritual enactment. The Robinsons, in ways described earlier, are able to sustain focused attention on the meal and one another.

The Exit Phase

The exit phase is the manner in which we leave ritual space, how we transition back into less focused family interaction. At church, the exit phase is marked by brief final words from the minister or priest and a concluding hymn. The congregation slowly files out of the church, perhaps resuming the hushed tones of the transition phase, and then returns to everyday talk in the public areas. The Hovlands, of course, do not have an exit phase. The D'Antonios wait until everyone is finished before concluding the meal—there is a clear exit phase—but sometimes it ends with scolding one of the children for not finishing the meal. Ending a family ritual on a negative note sours the experience. It would be like a minister ending the service by rebuking the congregation for not putting enough money in the collection basket. The Moores, who watch television during dinner, tend to drift away from the table as various individuals finish their food, thus not having a clear exit or closure to the meal. The Robinsons have not ritualized the exit phase very clearly, but wait until everyone is finished, whereupon one of the adults indicates that the meal over.

The intentional approach the Robinsons take to managing the phases of their family dinners may seem impossibly structured and overorganized to some families, but bear in mind that their meal ritual evolved slowly over time. When Cathy and Joe got married, they enjoyed having meals as a couple every night, highlighted by a special meal with wine at home on Saturday nights. When they had children, they continued with basic family meals, except on Saturday nights when they would feed the children first and try (often unsuccessfully) to have a meal for just the two of them after the children went to bed. It was when the children became preschoolers that the family began experimenting with candles, soft lighting, and music—all of which were a hit with the children. The parents stumbled for several years, by arguing excessively with the children about food, until they realized that the arguments were not helping their children's nutrition and were hurting the quality of family meals. In the past year, the second child has gone away to college, leaving Joe and Cathy back to their meals together—which they still do with candles, music, soft lights, and the door closed to the kitchen. Why abandon a good ritual because the kids are not around to enjoy it?

ELEMENTS OF INTENTIONAL FAMILY MEALS

I recommend family meals as the best place to begin the process of becoming more intentional as a family. Eating is a biological function that humans generally need to do three times a day. Children need to be fed by their parents, and most adults enjoy company while they eat their main meal of the day. For simplicity, the following discussion centers on family dinners, but the principles apply to other meals as well. Some families' schedules during the work week simply do not allow for many family dinners together, but they figure out how to ritualize breakfast or weekend dinners or Sunday brunches. The idea is to start from where you are and take a few small steps toward enhancing your family's meal rituals.

Here are the main elements of family meals you can work with, framed as questions to ask yourself about your family. Think about how each element currently works for your family, and which ones you want to modify. My comments are intended as suggestions, not as mandates, even if I say them strongly. The goal is to become more intentional, more planful, in order to have your meals reflect what *you* want for *your* family.

- *Who does the meal planning?* Unless one family member loves doing all the planning and shopping, it is best to have the involvement of other family members. Women often bear this burden alone. A good rule of thumb for family rituals is that the more people involved in planning it, the better the ritual is likely to be.
- *Who prepares the meal and sets the table?* Same idea as for planning. The burden on one person to please diverse family tastes can undermine that person's enthusiasm for the meal ritual. Some adults share the meal preparation and involve the children more actively as they become older. Even very young children can help set the table. Many people have warm childhood memories of working side by side with their mother preparing family meals, but there are no fixed rules about sharing the cooking. One couple with a three-year-old has a mutually satisfying arrangement whereby the father is responsible for picking up the child from day care and getting him home and settled (a 30-minute process), while the mother has quiet time to prepare the family meal.
- *Is the environment conducive to connection and conversation?* This is where creating a separate ritual space comes in. Even if you don't have a separate dining room, you can create ritual space in the kitchen by using candles and music. A dimmer switch for the lighting costs only a few dollars. The television should be off if family connection is the goal. Taking newspapers, bills, and lunchboxes off the table helps as well.
- *When is the meal served?* Predictability enhances the likelihood of a smooth transition to the meal. This does not necessarily mean the same time every night, if schedules don't permit

this. But it means *predictability*, knowing in advance each day when you will be eating that evening. One of the main obstacles to family meals is unpredictable work and school schedules. Being intentional about family meals means exercising control over work schedules. Generally, people manage to get home for high-priority family events, and if family meals are put in that category, family members will get home on time most of the time. Another time obstacle is the children's activity schedules and, later, their work schedules. Once again, Intentional Families find a balance between individual and family needs.

• *How are family members called to table?* Some families routinely start their meals on a negative note when the parents have to call repeatedly to the children to come to dinner, the last call often as a threat. Families with a fixed mealtime avoid this problem to some degree, but still must make the final call. One device my wife and I developed was to ring a bell five minutes before the meal was to start. It precluded having to locate the children, calling loudly upstairs or in the lower level of the house, and then listening for their sometimes muffled response. Since we knew that everyone in the house could hear the bell, ringing it sufficed.

• *Who is present?* Everyone, if possible. And even when someone is not, it is best to carry on with the regular family meal ritual instead of forgoing them for the day. Some families allow adolescent children to absent themselves from family meals if they are not hungry or in a bad mood. This is a serious mistake. It communicates to the adolescent that he or she has no obligations to the family. Better to have a pouting child present at the meal than an absent and aloof child. Similarly, if the family has young adult children living at home and on their own schedules, it is important to have an understanding that they will participate in some family meals. Otherwise, they can feel like boarders and not like family.

• *How are family members seated?* Families differ here. Some have regularly "assigned" seats (though often no one can remember how the assignments were made), while others have free-form seating. I suspect that Intentional Families tend toward more structure in the seating. One family with two school-age children has each child sit next to and across from a parent so that squabbling is minimized and both children have equal access to their parents.

• *What kinds of food are served?* One of the ways to signal a special dinner is to prepare a special meal. In my own family, my Sunday night spaghetti has always been a special meal, looked forward to during the day. Similarly, my wife's Danish pancakes have been a special brunch meal.

• *Are distractions and interruptions permitted?* In addition to the distractions of television and newspapers, the telephone can interrupt conversation or take a family member away for the whole meal. The value of the family meal can be demonstrated either by turning on the answering machine or politely telling callers that dinnertime is not a good time to talk.

• *What topics of conversation are encouraged?* Some families are very intentional about what they discuss at family meals. One family has each adult and child say something about what happened to them during the day. Some parents deliberately bring up issues of importance in the wider world or community. It can be helpful to think about the content of your meal conversations, and ask yourself whether you would like to consciously expand your repertoire.

• *What topics of conversation are discouraged?* As mentioned before, some parents deliberately avoid disciplinary conversations with children at meals, unless the child is misbehaving during the meal itself. Similarly, it is best to postpone marital conflicts until later.

• *Who participates in the conversations?* Does one person dominate the dinner talk, and is another uncommunicative? If so, you can devise strategies for changing the balance. One stepfather found himself consistently out of the conversational loop at dinner because one of his stepdaughters wouldn't talk to him. He and his wife decided that she would help him get conversation air time by addressing him directly more often, rather than just having a free-form family discussion that too often left him out.

• *How do you handle table manners and food preference issues with children?* As mentioned before, these are thorny topics for parents. A certain amount of instruction about eating etiquette and nutrition is a necessary part of family meals. But this is best kept to the minimum and done with firmness but not anger. It is important that both parents agree on the standards and participate in these conversations.

• *Is the end of the meal ritual clearly defined?* If family members leave the table on their own, the meal ritual degenerates rather than concludes. The adults, rather than the children, should signal the end of the meal. If the children are finished and the adults are lingering, the children should ask to be excused.

Keeping Meal Rituals Flexible

Being intentional about meal rituals sometimes means throwing out your structure. The highly ritualized Robinson family sometimes watches *60 Minutes* while eating its traditional spaghetti dinner on Sunday nights. And every four years, they prioritize the Olympics over all family meal discussions. And when Joe is out of town, Cathy and the children generally eat pick-up meals in the kitchen, sometimes with the television on. When neither of the Robinson adults has time to purchase and prepare a meal, they join 60 percent of American families who sometimes eat carry-out food for their family meal, which, by the way, can be ritualized, too.[4]

Inflexible family meal rituals can become oppressive. But Intentional Families like the Robinsons also know how to return to their family meal rituals after these breaks from routine so as not to let them disperse in the inviting waters of spontaneity. When their second child left for college, Joe and Cathy Robinson went through a phase either of eating out or eating at home in the kitchen, often with the evening news on. They behaved like liberated college kids themselves. Then they began to notice that they were not connecting at the end of the workday. Their dinners had become free-form and spontaneous, unlike their structured past, but were not meeting deeper needs. Joe and Cathy decided to return to the dining room and maintain the family meal ritual intact, allowing for spontaneous exceptions as they had in the past.

The Robinsons' dinner ritual experience demonstrates three important lessons: that highly ritualized family meals tend to be more satisfying, that flexibility is needed to keep these rituals from becoming oppressive, and that even Intentional Families never become immune to the pull of entropy.

FEELING GUILTY ABOUT FAMILY MEALS

The process of ritualizing family meals can feel overwhelming if currently you are lucky to scratch together anything in the evening, and if watching *Sesame Street* on television seems to be the only way to keep your toddler from throwing her food.

Do you return home late most nights?

Are you a single mother who can't tend to your kids and orchestrate a sublime dinner ritual—unless you take the day off from work?

Are you a stepfather whose adolescent stepchildren don't want to eat with you anyway?

Is a special family dinner take-out food that everyone is willing to eat on paper plates without complaining?

There are three general responses to these questions. First, there is no law that says you have to ritualize your family meals. You might just decide to keep daily meals as they are for now, and try out different rituals for bedtime, going out, birthdays, or other special occasions.

Second, you might try just one small change in your routine, such as asking everyone who is at home to sit down at the same table at the same time. If you often buy take-out food, you can still set a table as if you had prepared it yourself. Lighting a candle or saying a prayer does not require much extra time or energy. One family I know found that its three-year-old dinner terrorist went into a trance once the candle was lit and stayed in her chair in order to win the privilege of blowing it out at the end of the meal.

Third, if the members of your family are scattered during mealtimes, you might arrange for just one ritualized meal per week, as one single parent did with her on-the-go adolescent son. Small starts such as these can give your family a sense of the possibilities of meal rituals.

If you are concerned about how other family members would respond to even a simple suggestion for improving your meal ritual, I recommend that you bring it up as something you personally would like to try. Avoid direct criticism of how the family is eating its meals, as in "Our family meals are chaos, and nobody except me seems to care." You are sure to be met with defensive resistance, such as "What's wrong with the way we eat? And please don't stand in front of the television." One constructive technique is to simply make a small change yourself, such as lighting a candle or putting on music, and seeing how the others like it. Another is to follow a successful ritualized meal such as a Thanksgiving dinner with the suggestion that the family carry over some elements of that meal to everyday dinners. Example: "You know, it was really nice to wait until everyone was finished their meal before anyone left the table. How would you feel about trying that everyday? Would it make it feel more like a family meal?" Making ritual changes can be tricky, however. I recommend that you read the last chapter of this book before trying to make serious reforms in your family meals—or your efforts may backfire.

The hallmark of everyday family life is that families feed their members. In the face of the obstacles and distractions of modern life, Intentional Families find a way to use meals to feed their souls along with their bodies. It isn't easy, and it takes lots of trial and error, but even small enhancements of family meal rituals can have big payoffs in the form of improved family connections.

Rising and Retiring, Coming and Going

OUR ANCESTORS NO DOUBT would be amazed by how scheduled we have become. Throughout most of human history, families rose and retired pretty much with the sun. Precise hours during the day were not demarcated until mechanical clocks were invented by Benedictine monks in the Middle Ages. There was little pressure to be anywhere at a specific time in the morning, because no one knew exactly what time it was! And since many families had but one small room for sleeping, the nightly ritual of putting children to bed by themselves at a fixed hour presumably did not exist. Today, however, for better and for worse, the tyranny of the daily schedule gives us plentiful opportunities both for family connection and family conflict.[1]

RISE AND SHINE

Curt Russell hates weekday mornings when he is in charge of getting three children out of bed and off to school. His wife, Sandy, who works the early shift as a medical technician at the local hospital, leaves for work before Curt's alarm clock goes off at 6:30 A.M. The following scenario, as if carefully scripted, recurs almost daily:

> Curt opens the doors to the children's bedrooms and calls to wake them up.

Curt takes a quick shower and returns to the children's rooms and calls to them again, this time more loudly, to get out of bed.

Brandon (age 3) is generally up by this point and is either begging his father for special pancakes, or claiming he is not hungry at all. Either Michele (age 7) or Stacey (age 5) is lagging in bed, claiming to be too tired or too sick to get up. Curt moves back and forth between the kitchen ("No, Brandon, you can have cereal but not blueberry pancakes") and the girls' rooms, his temper rising.

A fight breaks out in the bathroom between the girls over the use of the toothpaste and the sink.

All three children are finally eating breakfast, but Stacey is dawdling over her cereal. Curt gets Brandon dressed after a brief battle over whether he can wear his favorite shirt for the third day in a row. The school bus is due to arrive for Stacey and Michele in five minutes.

Curt implores Stacey to finish her Frosted Flakes (nutrition was an early casualty of the Russell family's morning routines). She begins to eat even more slowly. Curt takes away her bowl and orders her to the bedroom where he has laid out her clothes. He stands over her until she is dressed.

Michele is waiting at the front door without her winter coat on, even though it's 10 degrees outside. An argument ensues about which coat she must wear; in exasperation, she throws her fall coat on the floor and reluctantly takes her heavy one out of the closet.

As the bus approaches, Curt quickly zips Stacey's coat and practically pushes her and Michele out, followed by hurried good-byes.

Curt helps Brandon on with his coat and drives him to the day-care center; and after a quick good-bye hug, Curt drives off to work at the lumberyard. It's a relief to him to get to work!

Most parents can identify with Curt's morning from hell. It is just part of being a parent. The problem is that this kind of routine can quickly become the norm. I say "routine" because the Russell's morning madness does not qualify as a family ritual. Although it is often repeated, it is far from coordinated and certainly does not have a positive outcome or significance. The Russells have a negative morning routine rather than a positive family ritual.

The Miller family, whom I saw in therapy for the parents' marital problems, had a morning routine not unlike the Russell's. The father, Sam, left for work before the others were up. The mother, Ruth, would sleep until the last minute before waking their daughters, ages 6 and 4. In addition to being frustrated with the children, Ruth was resentful of Sam for leaving early every morning. Sam admitted in therapy that he left for work earlier than necessary in order to avoid the chaos and conflict. Consequently, Ruth was always frazzled and angry by the time the children were out of the house and she was off to work.

Where to Begin

Although Ruth and Sam had a number of other serious problems—money, sex, in-laws, poor problem-solving skills—I decided to begin with their morning routine, which was a less stressful place to experiment with change. I asked about their morning routines *before* they had children. In contrast to the current situation, they would get up at the same time, have coffee and breakfast together, and discuss plans for the day. When I inquired about their work schedules at that time, Ruth smiled and said that she had always gone to work later than Sam, but had voluntarily gotten up earlier to be with him in the mornings. Sam remarked that he had enjoyed her company during that quiet time.

During this same therapy session, Ruth spontaneously offered to get up 20 minutes earlier to have breakfast with Sam. He volunteered to get the coffee going, to have it ready for her, as he used to do. Thus, they settled on the "transition phase" of a morning rit-ual—as opposed to routine. I then inquired how they wanted to use those 20 minutes. Did they want to talk, read the paper, watch *The Today Show?* This question triggered a memory for Ruth, that she would sometimes feel resentful when Sam was involved in his newspaper and did not listen or respond to her. But she also said that she enjoyed quietly reading the paper in the morning.

From those revelations, I helped them clarify their expecta-tions for the "enactment phase" of their morning ritual. Al-though they should feel free to look at the newspaper during their breakfast, their higher priority would be talking and con-necting, generally about plans for the day. This was a good com-promise, that gave them the flexibility to relax but ensured that conversation would always take precedence over the paper, if one of them had something to say.

From Negative Routine to Positive Ritual

The "exit phase" of Ruth and Sam's morning ritual of course had to include the beginning of the parent-child ritual. Sam reck-oned that he had more time flexibility in the mornings than he had admitted in the past, and volunteered to do the first round of getting the children out of bed and into the bathroom, while Ruth got herself dressed. He would then say good-bye to Ruth and the children, and head to work. With my coaching, Ruth de-cided to make the children's morning routine more or-derly: She laid their clothes out the night before, stayed with them until they were up and in the bathroom, and started preparing more spe-

> You can't be sure a ritual has taken root, until it has survived episodes of neglect.

cial breakfasts to make getting ready more attractive to the girls. And the more orderly pace allowed for more conversation.

The Russells thus transformed a negative family routine into a positive family ritual. This road was not without bumps and detours, however, because of other, separate, marital issues and because new rituals of connection do not take root immediately. For example, when for several days Sam again had to leave early for work, they fell back into their old habits—Ruth slept in until the last minute, and Sam did not wake her up to join him. The children were hassled. The forces of entropy threatened to take over.

Ruth and Sam had reached a critical phase in making this new ritual part of their family life. You can't be sure a ritual has taken root, until it has survived episodes of neglect. When I asked them if they both wanted to reinstate their morning connection ritual, they reaffirmed their commitment to it, and were subsequently able to follow through most of the time. In terms of their marital therapy, the positive time together and the sense that they could be intentional about their family life gave them an important boost to dealing with their other marital issues.

> Intentional Families don't necessarily ritualize every aspect of their life.

Intentional Families don't necessarily ritualize every aspect of their life. My own family, which is fairly intentional, does not ritualize mornings. I am task- rather than relationship-oriented in the mornings, and my wife's often-stated motto is: "I don't do mornings." When our children were young, our goal was an orderly rising, eating, and departure, with minimum fuss—and minimum conversation. Often, I was in charge because my wife worked an early shift at the hospital. At some point, I taught the children to use alarm clocks to awaken themselves, and to pour their own cereal and milk. As they became teenagers, I even declined to call them if they overslept; I felt it was their responsibility to set their alarms and make the school bus. They were late a few times, but not very often. Overall, weekday mornings were low in contact and low in conflict—a neutral rather than a negative routine or a positive ritual of connection. Weekend mornings were sometimes different, with a special pancake or waffle meal and an extended family discussion. But these were not frequent or predictable enough to qualify as a Doherty family ritual.

The final element of family morning routines and rituals is saying good-bye for the day. Emily Jones, a low-income single mother, does not always feel good about how hassled she is getting her children off to Head Start and elementary school, but she is proud of the fact that she always, without fail, hugs each child and says "I love you" as she sends them off. Emily completes this ritual no matter how badly the morning went, no matter how difficult the children have been, and no matter how she is feeling personally. *Consistency is at the heart of family rituals.*

Nor do connection rituals always need much in the way of words. Steve, a father of two preschool daughters, leaves for work before anyone else in the family is awake. For his departure ritual, he quietly goes into his daughters' rooms and adjusts their covers to make sure they are warm, then returns to the main bedroom to gently kiss his wife on the cheek, pretending not to wake her. She softly says, "Drive safely." Steve's children will cherish this ritual as they grow older. And his wife already does.

TAKE ME HOME, COUNTRY ROAD

Late afternoon is the "arsenic" hour for most American families with children. The adults are tired and hassled; the children are tired, irritable, and hungry. There is dinner to be made, mail to be looked through, schoolwork to be done, transportation to be arranged, the house to be picked up, sibling battles to be waged. Generally, one parent is alone for much of this, and upon arrival the other is then greeted with tension. Given all these challenges, many families do not ritualize their reconnection at the end of the workday. And they are missing an important opportunity.

Martha, a single parent who has arranged her work schedule to be home when her two school-age children return home, has created a satisfying ritual of daily reunion. She prepares them a snack and then spends a few minutes talking with each child about the day and going through materials they have brought home from school. After 10 to 15 minutes, the children head off to play. Lots of parents do this on occasion. What makes Martha's

a true ritual is her faithfulness to it and her planful approach to the conversation with the children. She does not let herself be distracted by Oprah Winfrey or by telephone calls or the mail. She gives the children her undivided attention and checks in with them as they eat their snack. She has also negotiated with the children the kinds of snacks they may have—they alternate between fruit and cookies or other sweets—so that there is little conflict over food. Not planning ahead in this way frequently leads to an initial power struggle between parent and child over the snack. When this happens, the transition phase into the connection ritual is ruined, and the likelihood of emotional bonding diminished.

Separate But Equal

Emily Jones, the woman who always says "I love you" before departing in the morning, also has an effective reconnection ritual with her daughter after she picks her up from the Head Start program. During their 10-minute walk from the child-care center to their house, they ask each other the same question every day: "What did you like about your day?" They talk for the whole walk, and then go about their separate activities when they walk in the door.

After school was when my wife Leah always enacted an important ritual of connection with our children. Her work schedule enabled her to be home before the children. She valued the discussions about their day and their plans; this was "Mom" time. If I happened to be around at that hour, which was infrequent, my presence interfered with the ritual, because I would talk to Leah or read the mail or ask the children the same questions she had just asked. My point is, when it comes to certain parent-child rituals, three's a crowd. Thus, I did bedtime; Leah did coming home.

While some families do a good job with homecoming rituals for the children, the parents sometimes neglect their own daily ritual of reunion. Roberta and Patrick Lynch had become a child-

centered couple over the years, to the neglect of their marriage. Roberta was a homemaker, caring for five children ranging from a first grader to a teenager. She was nearly always home to greet and spend time with each child after school. In fact, she liked this ritual so much that she had trouble accepting when her son Richard, a teenager, was no longer interested in chatting with her on many

> Most family connection rituals have to change as children get older.

days. (The family was in therapy because of problems with Richard.) This dilemma illustrates another important principle of family rituals: Most family connection rituals have to change as children get older. It was still important for Roberta to be available for Richard at the end of the day, and to inquire about his day, but she had to accept his need for privacy.

Two's Company

Patrick, Roberta's husband, had a positive reentry ritual when he returned home from work about 5:30 P.M. every day. He would first greet the dog, always the most eager creature in the house. Then he would greet each child individually, connecting with five children and one canine—but, significantly, not his wife, who generally stayed in the kitchen at this time. Patrick would then change clothes and putter about the house. When they finally ended up in the same room with each other—often when Patrick came into the kitchen—they would take up a conversation about some household matter. But they had no ritualized way to greet each other.

When I inquired of Roberta and Patrick how they felt about their reunion routine, Patrick said he had not thought about it, and Roberta said she felt sad about it. She was more conscious that their reentry routines symbolized distance in the relationship, but she had not said anything to her husband or tried to change the pattern. When I asked what they had done early in their marriage before they had children, they both admitted that they had warmly greeted each other with a hug and kiss and a question about how the other's day had been.

I then asked the next logical question: "How would you feel about returning to the reunion ritual of your earlier years?" This produced embarrassed laughs from both of the them. It was hard for them to think about being that intimate in front of the children. The children would faint, Roberta believed. And they wondered whose responsibility it would be to initiate the greeting? What if one offered a kiss and the other turned away? Although Roberta and Patrick still had an adequate sexual relationship, despite other problems, this everyday connection felt new and risky to them.

I encouraged them to negotiate exact steps for the ritual. Here is what they came up with:

> After greeting the dog and the kids, Richard would proceed to the kitchen where Roberta was working.
>
> They would simultaneously greet each other; he would approach her, and they would exchange a hug and a kiss on the cheek. The cheek was a safer place to start than the lips, Roberta felt.

Even this simple ritual took many weeks to institute on a regular basis, because they feared rejection and because they had not consciously worked on their relationship in many years. Becoming intentional after years of inertia does not happen without a struggle.

I have worked with less troubled couples who had a similar greeting pattern, even those without children in the home. In one household, the one entering the house last would call out "Hello"; the other spouse would yell "Hello" from somewhere in the house. The person who had just come in would then change clothes and attend to household matters. Unlike the Lynches, this couple acknowledged the other's presence in the home, even though their reunion routine was minimal—they had no face-to-face connection until they wandered into each other's presence; and even then, no warm greeting or touching was exchanged. Upon reflecting on how they seemed to be taking each other for granted in a number of ways, they decided on the following ritual: Whoever was home first would come to the entryway to greet the other; they would exchange a hug and kiss, and then spend a few minutes checking in about their respective days.

Reentry after a day apart is a crucial moment for families. Intentional Families can't always avoid the stress and hassle of "arsenic hour," but they can find ways to create positive rituals of connection that jump-start them toward a positive evening. Families with dogs can learn something from their companion animals: Each day, without exception, most dogs engage in a charming rebonding ritual with the humans they love.

TO SLEEP, PERCHANCE TO DREAM

Bedtime struggles between parents and children are legendary. Parents mandate something that used to occur spontaneously, before civilization took control over the hours of the day.[2] We assume that children's biological clocks correspond to our social clocks, to our sense of when they should sleep. Trust me, I am not arguing for a laissez-faire bedtime for families, because most children need their sleep, and because parents need time without child-care responsibilities. But it takes a fair amount of ritual creativity to make something positive out of an inherently conflictual time in the evening.

Setting the Time for Bedtime

Since predictability is a hallmark of a ritual, it is important to establish a clear bedtime for children, at least until the teen years. Periodic renegotiations of a later time are of course warranted, but continual debate over bedtime erodes the possibility of parent-child connection during the ritual. Therefore, the time should be set and made clear to the child; younger ones who cannot tell time should be given notice well in advance of the start of the transition to bed. Unnecessary family conflicts ensue when parents are too flexible with bedtimes, or let the child decide every night, because there will inevitably be disagreements and debates.

The bedtime transition phase is particularly important for young children. Every experienced parent knows that you have to begin the process well in advance of the child's actually getting under the bed covers. This phase may begin with bath and pajamas, and perhaps a snack or cuddle time on the sofa. No roughhousing or loud noises. Not organizing the transition phase early enough creates a sense of rush later, which undermines the ritual potential of bedtime.

Storytime

If all goes well in the transition phase, the high point of bedtime is likely to be one-to-one time between a parent and child. This ritual often involves stories or talk. This was my favorite ritual with my children. We tended to combine books and talk in their younger years, and then just talked as they got older. Children love the ritual of a parent reading them a favorite story over and over. For my kids, it was *George the Baby-Sitter*, about the travails of a teenage boy baby-sitting for two rambunctious children. Another favorite activity was hide and seek with the bed covers. Even our conversations tended to be ritualized, covering the same territory and laughing at the same lines: Beth: "I'm hot." Dad: "I thought you were Beth." Beth: "No, I *feel* hot!" My kids jealously guarded their bedtime talks. My daughter would count the number of minutes I spent with her brother and remind me if I tried to terminate our talk prematurely.

I hated to see bedtime rituals end with my children. I remember when my son was about 13 and said two nights in a row that he didn't want to talk that night. The second time I asked, "Shall we leave it that you ask me if you want to talk?" I knew it was over. I found my wife downstairs, and cried. When my daughter reached the same age, the transition was easier. I had been let-ting her take the initiative for bedtime talks for some months, and after a long family vacation, she did not initiate them again. (In the next chapter, I describe the ritual we replaced it with.)

Following the bedtime story or talk, most parents kiss their child; some say "I love you," and some parents say a prayer with their child. The exit from the ritual occurs with the child tucked in bed and the parent leaving the room. If there is a struggle at this stage on a regular basis, it casts a pall over the whole bed-time ritual. The smartest parents, in my observation, do not command their child to go to sleep right away (who can fall asleep on command?), but allow them to read or play quietly in their room with the door closed. Whatever the final injunction to the child, the key is that the ritual end without a struggle. Chil-dren who leave their room, unless there is a problem, should be calmly but firmly escorted back to their bed. Again, post good-night conflict cripples subsequent bedtime rituals because both parent and child will be anxious about what might follow the goodnight kiss.

Avoiding the Parent Trap

In two-parent families, the parents have to figure out who does the bedtime rituals with which children on which nights. If the parents do not work this out amicably and fairly, the ritual will be disrupted; the child will sense something is wrong, or the parent will not have his or her heart in the ritual. Given the greater responsibility most mothers feel for daily caregiving, un-less a couple is intentional about bedtime, the mother will end up doing the lion's share. I believe this is often a mistake, espe-cially if the mother already has more one-to-one time with the children than the father and is tired of child care by the end of the day. I recommend that fathers, whenever possible, take over the entire bedtime ritual from baths onward. Or, if the mother wants to share in this ritual, I recommend that the parents split the days equally. Either way, it is crucial that children know that either of their parents can connect with them through a bedtime ritual. Children who expect or demand to be put to bed by one parent (usually the mother) begin to control that part of the day too much, and miss out on the advantage of connecting with two loving parents.

In addition to sharing the ritual as much as possible, parents should agree on all the ground rules: time to start the bedtime process, bath rules (how often, when to shampoo, and so on), whether a snack is permitted, whether exceptions can be made to tooth brushing, whether the child can come out of the room to ask questions or make requests. The ritual works best when both parents generate these rules, agree to them, communicate them to the child, and enforce them. The main challenge in two-parent families is consistency between the parents.

In single-parent families, the challenge for the lone adult during bedtime rituals is to be tenacious. I recommend that you remind yourself that bedtime rules create opportunities for parent-child bonding, for meeting your child's needs, and for giving you needed time to yourself. These are not arbitrary restrictions on your child's freedom (an argument your child is likely to make).

In remarried families, the key is for the stepparent to support the bedtime policies of the biological parent, and for the biological parent to be sensitive to the stepparent's needs when setting those policies. Generally, the children will want their original parent to manage bedtime rituals and rules, at least in the early years of the remarriage. The stepparent can provide moral support to his or her spouse to help make bedtime orderly and bonding.

GOOD NIGHT, MY SWEET

Going to bed together is one of the defining activities of a married or a cohabiting couple. "Sleeping together," after all, is a euphemism for having a sexual relationship. Young people contemplating marriage regard this as the high point of the day for a married couple, the time of close connection and romantic potential. Newlyweds, who often view bedtime as a central focus in their relationship, have trouble imagining that they might someday have to be intentional about maintaining that aspect of their marriage. Yet the reality is that many couples, particularly after they have children, lose the connection with each other at the end of their day.

Relieved to be in a happy second marriage, Lois and Ed had always gone to bed together, after getting Lois' two girls tucked in, the laundry finished, the bills paid, the house picked up, and the news watched. But after the children left home, Lois and Ed found themselves drifting into a different nightly pattern. Lois would sometimes stay up late to work on a project; or Ed would work on his computer. Their morning schedules were not as hectic, which gave them more flexibility to stay up later at night. Gradually, though, they found themselves going to bed separately more often than together.

What did Lois and Ed lose? The opportunity to talk, cuddle, and sometimes have sexual relations. And although their day together always ended with a goodnight and a kiss, it's not the same as lying in bed together. After attending a family rituals workshop, Lois began to realize what she and Ed were missing, and decided to talk to him about it.

Mary and Frank relinquished their bedtime ritual much sooner in their marriage than Lois and Ed, the familiar casualty of having babies and young children. In addition, Mary and Frank had different sleep needs. Mary was usually exhausted by 9:30 P.M., when Frank was getting his second wind. She would crawl off to bed, and he would roam the house until after midnight. They didn't make a conscious choice to get into this nightly pattern, but both admitted to feeling less connected because of it.

When Mary and Frank's bedtime routine came up during couple's therapy, I learned that they argued about it at home. Mary would complain that Frank never came to bed with her, and Frank would argue that he couldn't go to sleep when she did. She would try to stay up later, but then be exhausted; he would sometimes come to bed with her, but then complain that he could not sleep. In the therapy, I helped them to accept their different sleep patterns at this time in their lives, and asked them to describe what they felt they were missing by not going to bed together.

I then coached them to agree that most nights they would both get into bed around 10 o'clock to spend some time cuddling and talking. Mary would then go to sleep and Frank would be free to get up to spend time on his own if he preferred. They both realized the issue was not whether they went to sleep at the same time, but whether they went to bed together in order to connect. The ritual change worked fairly well for Mary and Frank, although when other marital problems surfaced they found themselves "forgetting" to go to bed together. We then had to talk about the unequal division of child care and housework responsibilities, which contributed to Mary's exhaustion.

Good rituals are not a panacea for family problems that must be worked through separately, but they can keep families from drifting farther apart while they work on their problems. Even couples who generally go to bed together can benefit from being more intentional about this ritual. One of the major distractions from communicating at bedtime is the television, which, according to a Gallup poll, can be found in an astonishing 80 percent of American bedrooms![3] While many couples no doubt find it relaxing to watch television together, this practice can also impact on conversation and attention to each other. It can also be a soporific that brings on sleep before conversations or sexual desires have a chance to surface.

The Intentional Couple pays careful attention to bedtime rituals. Most other connecting rituals can be shared with other family members and even friends, but sleeping together every night brings married couples together. That we tend to drift away from this unique and powerful ritual of connection is a testament to the power of entropy in intimate relationships. We must be intentional with rituals that once seemed so natural and necessary.

Going Out and Going Away

Wʜᴀᴛ ᴡᴇʀᴇ ʏᴏᴜʀ ꜰᴀᴠᴏʀɪᴛᴇ ꜰᴀᴍɪʟʏ ʀɪᴛᴜᴀʟꜱ as a child? Chances are that your list includes family outings. Many favorite family rituals occur on short or long trips. Family outings, whether to McDonald's or a vacation at the beach, focus the family's attention on common activities outside the daily household routines. Ironically, it's easier to minimize distractions at a restaurant or on a car ride than it is in the "wired" world of home. If yours is an underritualized family, going out is a good place to start becoming more intentional.

A few weeks after my daughter Elizabeth and I stopped having our bedtime talks, she suggested one evening that the two of us go to Dairy Queen for ice cream. During the car ride, we played our favorite "rhyme that name" game, inspired by the country-and-western song "Tequila Sheila." It was a word game we loved but one that drove her brother and mother up the wall; alone in the car, we could indulge ourselves in silly rhymes. At the restaurant, Elizabeth talked about her schoolteachers, her friends, and whatever else came to mind. Before we left, she suggested we take home ice cream for her brother and mother.

THIRD TIME'S THE CHARM

A ritual is not a ritual the first time you do something new; nor the second. My son liked to say that it's not a family tradition until the third time. I don't know exactly when Elizabeth and I decided we had a genuine father-daughter ritual on our hands, but we kept going to Dairy Queen once a week for over five years, until she left home at age 18. And we still do it from time to time when she returns home from college. Often, we went on Wednesday night, but the specific evening was flexible. It was always after dinner and kitchen cleanup; and we always offered to bring home ice cream for the others. Needless to say, on some January nights in Minnesota, we were the only customers at the Dairy Queen on Hennepin Avenue; in July, we had to wait in line with the fair-weather customers. We got to know the weeknight staff, especially Jeff, who would greet us and start our order as soon as we walked in (an M&M Blizzard for Elizabeth, a Hawaiian Breeze for me). We sat at the same table when it was available, and grumbled under our breaths when some trespasser had taken it.

Some nights at the DQ, Elizabeth had an agenda for us to talk about. Maybe she was having problems with one of her friends. Maybe something in social studies class had caught her interest. From early childhood, Elizabeth had been fascinated with the big questions: God, evolution, the human mind. Just the kinds of imponderables I enjoy expounding upon. Sometimes a more personal topic did not come up until we were driving home, and sometimes we didn't talk about anything personal or profound but just enjoyed each other's company.

Our DQ trips had all the elements of a family ritual. The transition phase began with by agreeing that we would go out that night, followed by making sure the dishes were finished, the kitchen was cleaned up, and orders for ice cream were taken from other family members. This phase ended when we got in the car, where the one-to-one ritual enactment phase began. We both knew, without saying it, that the goal was not so much ice cream as connection, although the ice cream gave a pleasurable excuse to be together when there was nothing

> The great thing about regular rituals of connection is that they are there; you don't need a special reason to get together.

special to talk about. The great thing about regular rituals of connection is that they are there; you don't need a special reason to get together.

The exit phase began with the drive home, when we sometimes listened to the radio instead of talking. We would often have a mock argument over which station to listen to—contemporary rock versus oldies. (Once, I used the exit phase to bring up a concern her mother and I had about her behavior—lack of follow-through on chores, as I recall. This was a mistake. What had been a pleasant ritual of connection degenerated into a standard parent-adolescent argument about responsibility. There was no good reason to have this discussion at this time, during a connection ritual. And it ruined the outing. I never made that mistake again. There is plenty of opportunity at home during a typical week to challenge a child's behavior. Rituals of connection serve other purposes.)

Arriving home signaled the exit phase of the father-daughter ritual of connection. When we entered the house, we resumed our separate evening routines: Elizabeth on the phone or doing homework, and I chatting with her mother or working on the computer.

LET'S EAT OUT

I never met a child who didn't like to eat out. For children, it's a break from routine and a chance to eat what they want. For the adults, too, it's a break not only from routine but from cooking and cleaning up. For everyone, the drive to the restaurant, the meal itself, and the drive home can serve as a family connection ritual, perhaps the most common family outing of all. And since families are eating out more often, it makes sense to turn this activity into a family ritual.

What does it take to turn lunch or dinner out into a family ritual? The act of having a meal out does not in and of itself make the activity a ritual, even though family members may enjoy it. It becomes a ritual when it is *repeated, coordinated, and significant*.

It's a ritual when it becomes part of the family's symbolic life, part of its identity.

The Walkers, a family with a good income, belong to a country club that has a minimum charge for eating in the restaurant each month; in other words, they charge members for the food whether they eat there or not. For many years, since their two children were small, the Walkers have eaten at the club's restaurant once a week. They enhance its value as a time of family connection by enacting the following ritual: Each family member has the spotlight for a few minutes to say something that happened to him or her that week. The mother, Denise, who had a gift for ritual, was the initiator and organizer of this ritual "check-in" during the meal. She would wait until everyone had ordered their food and then use the interval before the food arrived to orchestrate the connection ritual. Sometimes the check-in was fairly routine, but other times there was significant sharing by both parents and children, as when Jonathan, the 12-year-old, reported that he was aware that this was the third anniversary of the death of his grandfather. Without the ritual, no one would have known he was thinking about his grandfather. Or the time the father admitted that he had been cranky at home because of pressure at work. Absent that check-in ritual, he might never have said something that self-revealing.

Mary Hastings, a single parent with three preteen children, cannot afford a country club or a nice restaurant, but her family enjoys going out for pizza once a week. After moving to the Twin Cities a decade ago, they scouted around for a favorite restaurant, and chose Davanni's Pizza. Over time, they all realized that they were "committed" to Davanni's as part of their night out. (Mary learned this when she dragged the children to another pizza restaurant; nobody enjoyed it.) The family's outings became highly coordinated: Mary would call ahead for a pepperoni pizza and four soft drinks. The call signaled the time for everyone to get in the car—the only time in their family life, by the way, when there was no hassle in getting out the door in a timely fashion. At the restaurant, while Mary paid for the order, the two older children divided up the tasks of getting the plastic plates, utensils, and straws, and then setting the table. The third child waited with Mary to pick up the soft drinks. Everyone had regular seats at the family's favorite table, or a table near the favorite one. These moves became like a choreographed family dance, even though no one could remember how their dance routine started. Unlike the Walkers, the Hastings did not have a discussion procedure during their meal, but they often found themselves more engaged and attentive during their night out than they were during meals at home.

During the early months of their Davanni's pizza outings, one or more of the Hastings children would ask permission to play video games while waiting for the pizza to come out of the oven. At first, Mary allowed this, but soon realized that the distraction of the video games diminished the chance for family conversation. So she banned video games, and told the children that this was a time for being together as a family, not a time for separate activities such as video games. Mary protected the boundaries of an important family ritual, and said why. *If family members can come and go from a ritual, it loses its coordination and its opportunity for bonding.* Mary not only preserved the ritual but she educated her children about the importance of family ties.

ON THE ROAD AGAIN

My wife's favorite going-out ritual as a child was the Sunday drive with her family. After attending an early church service in their rural Iowa community, the family would pack a picnic lunch and head out of town. This ritual was both predictable and spontaneous. Predictable because they did it so frequently, especially in good weather, and because it generally involved a picnic lunch; spontaneous because sometimes they did not decide in advance where they would go. They might end up in another town at a park, or at an ice cream shop. Sometimes they would just drive. Along the way, her parents observed the farms

and towns, and commented about what was going on in the
Iowa countryside. What was special was that the family was together—parents and four children—spending a quiet Sunday
afternoon exploring their environment.

Camping becomes a part of some families' identity. If you talk
with them about what kind of family they are, you will soon hear
about camping trips. The Jorgenson family camped once or
twice a month in good weather from the time their son Joseph
was a toddler until he was an adolescent. In the early years, they
went to a local campground just a few miles from home, where
they loved the complete break from household routines. They
didn't do everything together on these trips: Al and Joseph would
often fish while Rae would catch up on her historical novels. But
they cooked and ate three meals together, they never brought a
radio or television, and they all enjoyed hiking. A favorite time of
day was sunset, when they would sit together at the campfire,
talking quietly, while Dad played his guitar.

When Joseph became school-age and appreciated more variety, the family began to travel farther away, and once a year they
took a family camping vaca-
tion. The parents sometimes
allowed Joseph to invite a
friend, but only someone they
knew well and who was al-
ready a part of their family in
some way. Other times the
family camped and vacationed
with other family members
and close friends, but these
experiences never replaced the
Jorgensons' time alone. Even
though Joseph eventually outgrew family camping, as most teenagers do, it had served its purpose as a connection ritual of his
childhood.

> The keys to making a going-out
> activity a genuine ritual are that
> family members do the activity
> together on a regular basis, that
> they know their roles and place
> in the activity, and that there is
> some feeling of connection.

Families devise innumerable going-out rituals to fit their
tastes: miniature golf, shopping at the mall, cross-country ski-

ing, fishing, boating, swimming, hiking, biking, walking around the neighborhood, going to the movies, or out for a meal or snack. Some involve money, and some are free or cheap. The keys to making a going-out activity a genuine ritual are that family members do the activity together on a regular basis, that they know their roles and place in the activity, and that there is some feeling of connection.

Upgrading Outings to Rituals

I suggest you inventory your favorite family outings, to see which of them already qualify as a family ritual and which of them you might want to turn into a family ritual. If an activity is already a ritual (repeated, coordinated, connecting) consider enhancing it in some way. For example, if going to movies regularly is an enjoyable family activity, you might want to enhance your family connection by having a discussion on the way home to find out what each member thought of the movie. If you play miniature golf, go out for a soft drink afterward and spend time talking as a family. If you go snowmobiling, incorporate a hot cocoa gathering at the end, rather than letting everyone just scatter.

The easiest way to start or upgrade family rituals of connection is to determine what you already enjoy doing as a family, and then do it more intentionally. If, like many American families, you go out for dinner regularly, give some thought to your favorite places and favorite food, and to those places that lend themselves to a pace slow enough for family conversation. (An advantage of pizza for the Hastings was that its preparation was slow enough, even with calling ahead, to afford time for conversation.) If walking through the park is something you occasionally enjoy, consider elevating it to ritual status by incorporating it regularly into your family's routine. A variety of regular family activities can become true rituals by doing them more frequently and in a more coordinated way, and by adding an opportunity for conversation.

WHO'S ON FIRST? THE FAMILY DYNAMICS OF GOING OUT

Some families do not ritualize going out because it requires leadership and cooperation, which are sometimes in short supply, resulting in less than positive experiences. Karen and Kent Browne, for example, argued whenever they went out with the children. They had trouble agreeing on which restaurant to go to, which shops to stop at on the way home, even whether to go out at all. Ironically, this couple was adept at making big decisions—having children, buying and selling their home, spending money—but they couldn't handle whether to go to Burger King or McDonald's. Their "game" could be titled "I'll Decide. No, I'll Decide." Their particular twist on the power struggle was that Karen claimed to be taking the children's interests into consideration, and Kent would assert that the children should accept whichever restaurant the parents chose. Surprisingly, the family did manage to eat out fairly regularly, but the parents were generally irritated with each other by the time they got there, because one of them had to "give in."

In a single-parent family, if the parent does not express a preference or actively structure the decision, but rather leaves the choice up to the children, a sibling power struggle may ensue. One child may threaten a boycott, saying "I won't eat at Bugger King." When the parent finally intervenes, one child is guaranteed to be unhappy and the going out ritual is probably ruined. This game is titled "If I Don't Get My Way, I Won't Go." Some adults are skilled at it as well.

Another going-out game couples play is the Alphonse and Gaston routine: "You Decide." "No, No, You Decide." These couples won't make up their minds because neither spouse is willing to express a preference, or be committed to a preference for very long. Here is how the conversation goes:

Wife: "Where would you like to eat?"

Husband: "I don't care. Where would *you* like to eat?"

Wife: "It really doesn't matter to me. *You* decide."

Husband: "I don't care either. I'll go where *you* want."

Wife: "Maybe we should just stay home."

Husband: "Whatever."

Another common and frustrating couple dynamic occurs when one spouse routinely initiates going-out decisions, and the other is agreeable, but won't initiate or express a personal preference. The game is: "You Decide For Me."

Wife: "How about we go out for dinner tonight?"

Husband: "Fine with me."

Wife: "Where would you like to eat?"

Husband: "I don't care."

Wife: "I'm always the one to pick the place. Why don't you decide tonight?"

Husband: "Why should I decide when I can eat anything?"

Wife: "But don't you have a preference?"

Husband: "I told you—I don't care."

Wife: (voice raised) "But I'm sick of always making the decisions about where we go."

Husband: (now irritated): "You're the one with the strong views around here. I'm easy."

Wife: "All right. We're going to Pizza Hut, but you pick the next time."

Husband: "Sure, if it'll make you happy."

All the preceding family dynamics cripple the possibility of a meaningful ritual. Imagine the challenge to families such as these of making a decision on a group vacation.

Changing the Dynamics

Often these families either don't go on vacation, or someone sabotages the good time because of the power struggle. One strategy to change these dynamics is to have a discussion outside of the context of a particular instance of going out about how the couple or family is handling its going-out rituals. Whoever starts the discussion should be prepared not to blame others, but focus instead on improving the family's going-out rituals.

An intervention that therapists sometimes use to help families who can't make joint decisions is the every-other-time strategy: In a couple, the wife and husband agree to alternate who proposes where they will go for their outing; the other spouse agrees in advance to be open to that suggestion unless there is a strong countervailing reason. If the children are making the decision (within a range of parent-approved places), they too can alternate between themselves who decides where the family will go. Or the family can simply alternate which restaurant it goes to among the favorites.

But if going-out problems are symptomatic of deeper family struggles, these solutions often will not work because family members will not be able to cooperate, in which case, consultation with a family therapist might be needed.

THE ENDLESS HIGHWAY: FAMILY VACATIONS

Although family vacations actually constitute a small segment of time in the years of childhood, they tend to loom large in adult memories. I remember clearly the vacations my family spent at Wildwood, New Jersey, when I was a child: the apartment we always rented, our walks to the beach, the cool sand under the boardwalk where we settled in order to keep our Irish skin from blistering, playing "shark" with my father in the ocean, killing mosquitoes before we went to bed. Vacation memories endure because they occur in "a time out of time."

Interestingly, for all their significance to memories and family connection, family vacations are a recent phenomenon in human history, at least for all but the very wealthy. They became popular in the twentieth century, with the advent of paid time off from work. Like other rituals, family vacations sometimes evolve in ways that do not promote positive family connections. They can be misused as a status symbol, as in "We can afford two weeks at Disney World." Children may be taken to destinations of interest only to the parents, say, the battlefields of the Civil War, with little regard for the children's interests or family bonding. Or family holidays can be folded into trips to see extended family members, in which case they serve as a way to connect with the broader family but may preclude the chance for the nuclear family unit to enjoy each other and share new experiences. Family trips to see relatives don't necessarily constitute family vacations.

Making the Most of Vacation Time

Families are taking shorter vacations than they did in the past. The reasons are tied to our busy lifestyles and the fact that in most households both parents now work outside the home. Although most people imagine a family vacation as, at least, a week or two, currently, the average vacation is 4.7 nights. American workers are given far shorter paid vacations than most of the rest of the industrialized world. It is thus difficult to coordinate these short time periods with the schedules of two parents and the children's activities.[1] Needless to say, family vacations require more intentional thought and planning than ever before.

> The two principal challenges of family vacations are how to plan them and how to handle the concentrated time together.

The two principal challenges of family vacations are how to plan them and how to handle the concentrated time together. Planning requires not only attention to what the family can afford, but also to the competing needs and goals of different family members. The parents may want to go somewhere to relax after a busy work year, while the young children want to go to Sea World, and the adolescents want to scuba dive. A single mom might want to go antiquing, while her 12-year-old son wants to go river rafting. Stepdad wants to go to a golfing resort to sharpen his game, while the stepchildren want to go to their grandparents' lake cabin where they traditionally vacation. King Solomon would throw up his hands.

Planning Principles

The key planning principles are to discuss and consult with *all* family members, and to try to agree on a destination that satisfies more than one need—antiquing in a town near a lake, for example. It can also be helpful to sketch out plans for future vacations as well, so that family members who lose out this year will be assured that their turn will come. Stepdad will get his golfing vacation, but not this year. For families who go to the same spot each year, planning is not the problem, but protests may surface from teenagers who are bored going to the same place. Parents should be prepared to negotiate in good faith, but not just surrender the family's traditional vacation spot that has served the family well for many years.

Out of the Mouths of Babes

A major challenge for planning family vacations over the years is to keep the holidays consistent, but with enough flexibility to accommodate the children as they mature. An unchanging family vacation ritual—always the same place at the same time with the same people—runs the risk of becoming rigid and hollow. And allowing adolescent children to absent themselves from family vacations is not a good idea. It deprives them and the family of their final opportunities for this unique form of family bonding. Once children reach their teen years, the countdown begins to leaving home—or at least not wanting to be part of annual family vacations. It is worth doing some creative negotiating with adolescents to find a way for them to participate in family vacations without feeling like prisoners. A journalist who asked teens for tips that they would offer parents about family vacations, came up with the following list, which has a lot of good advice for parents of children of any age:

- *"Let us sleep."* Try to arrange the schedule so that teenagers can have some of their normal sleep-ins. Let them decline some morning activities.

- *"Compromise on culture."* Alternate a day at the Smithsonian with a day at the amusement park.

- *"Cut the lectures."* Avoid lengthy speeches about the historical sites along the way. A few sentences will suffice.

- *"Be casual."* Let them dress as they want, unless there is a pressing reason for specific attire.

- *"Pile on the food."* Decide in advance that you will be stopping frequently for snacks and meals. Vacation is not the time for a campaign to improve eating habits.[2]

But while being flexible, parents should also insist that children and adolescents participate in family activities. Catering too much to children can communicate the message that they're not really part of the group. One goal of a vacation is to share experiences with family, which means making compromises and being a good sport.

The second challenge, managing togetherness, is at the heart of the family vacation ritual. Closer family interactions also mean that people will get on one another's nerves more. *All lengthy family rituals involve irritability:* A family that perhaps rarely eats more than three meals together in a week now has three meals together in a day! The family car grows smaller and tighter with each passing mile. Fewer bedrooms and bathrooms mean less privacy. Long walks, hot days, strange food, dozens of decisions each day about what to do . . . need I say more? In everyday life, families maintain harmony partly by calibrating how much time they will spend in one another's presence. On vacation, these routines give way to unrelenting contact—which gives family vacations their charm, their dangers, and their opportunities for moments of both sweetness and frustration.[3]

A third challenge is to decide in advance the duties and responsibilities of each family member on the vacation. If the family is going to a cabin, how will cooking and cleaning and outdoor work be shared? If camping, who will put up the tent and gather the firewood? If visiting relatives, will time with family be shared equally or will the wife end up entertaining her mother-in-law again while the husband goes biking with his brothers? Generally speaking, the more coordinated the family roles are in advance of the vacation, the smoother this family ritual will be.

A great thing about family vacations is that after they're over, we soon forget the friction and irritability, and remember them fondly. We develop amnesia for the bad times, or we transform them into humorous family stories that give vacations a special place in family lore. When I was around 6, my father cut his foot on a shell at the beach. I remember riding with him in the back-end of the little truck that served as a makeshift ambulance for that beach, watching the trail of blood left on the sand as we drove. What stands out most about that experience is my father's often-recounted story of how the nurse told him to stop bleeding on the floor of the infirmary! "What do you think I'm here for?" my father retorted. The story of the cut, the nurse's amazing comment, and my father's response became one of the principal memories of our summer vacations at the beach. Even a family vacation ruined by a hurricane can become the most memorable vacation of them all—years later, of course.

In addition to recognizing that most of the minor irritations and tragedies of vacations will be whitewashed over the years, it is helpful to be creative to head off predictable problems. On our long car trips, for example, my wife came up with the rule that each of the children could ask only three times "When are we going to get there?"—a question that used to drive us crazy. The result was that they would save up their three shots, and then not always use them. We also learned to play family games in the car, such as locating as many different state license plates as possible, and playing word games that would take hours.

A family's going-out rituals, whether to the ice cream store or to the other end of the continent, are at the heart of a family's identity. They can profoundly define childhood memories of family life. They are when families have the most fun, the most vexation, and sometimes the most connection. They are an ideal place to start becoming a more intentional family.

CHAPTER

FIVE

Couple Rituals

Wᴇɴ ᴄᴏᴜᴘʟᴇꜱ ᴀʀᴇ ꜰᴀʟʟɪɴɢ ɪɴ ʟᴏᴠᴇ, they are experts at creating rituals. After they marry, they often lose their touch. Larry and Chris Murphy are good examples. They met on the dance floor, where friends thought them well matched for grace, good looks, and personality. Dancing became their love ritual, their regular time to enjoy each other as a couple. But by the time I saw them for therapy, they had a number of marital problems, the underlying of which was a sense of being emotionally disconnected from each other, and absorbed in their careers, in raising their child, and in running a household.

After hearing how they met, I asked whether they still went dancing. They confessed with embarrassment that they not been dancing for many years. "Why not?" I asked. Dancing was a singles activity, they thought; and after their son was born, they had no time anyway. Like the majority of couples, Larry and Chris abandoned and did not replace their courtship rituals when they settled into the serious business of marriage and parenthood.

Loving couples contemplating a permanent commitment cannot imagine that they will ever stop doing the activities that drew them together. If they love romantic dinners, they can't imagine forgoing them after they marry. Or they can't fathom giving up long walks, or back rubs in the evening, or burning incense when they make love, or sending each other love notes, or saying "I love you" whenever they say good-bye. These are the kinds of love rituals that turn two people into a couple—and then fail to survive the marriage.

Why? One important explanation for this troubling but familiar pattern is that courting couples generally are far more intentional than married couples. Couples who are falling in love and considering marriage make a priority of engaging in couple-oriented activities that help them feel close; for both parties, the relationship is a major project. In male-female romances, the man is likely to

> Courting couples generally are far more intentional than married couples.

be at his most attentive to the relationship, actively thinking about ways they can be together, about love rituals; and she is thinking the same way. Some of the luster dims for cohabiting couples after they begin living together, but they tend to be fairly intentional about their relationship if they are in the process of deciding whether to make a marital commitment.

THE MALE-FEMALE PROBLEM

In the early months and initial years of marriage, if the couple does not have children, their relationship usually has enough momentum so that the gradual slippage in love rituals may not be very noticeable. The relationship is still new, and spending time together is desirable and feels natural. They may still call each other every day at work to say hello and express affection. If they have a favorite song, they still play it. But even during this period before children, most couples

> Men tend to work consciously on an intimate relationship when pursuing a commitment or salvaging one.

become less intentional about couple rituals. The decline is often particularly apparent with the husband. Men tend to work consciously on an intimate relationship when pursuing a commitment or salvaging one. When the bond is well established, as in a stable marriage, many men are content to let the relationship evolve without a lot of focus and planning. For them, getting married is like buying a good new car: you research the best car you can afford, you make your best deal, and then hope you don't have to worry about any major repairs for at least 50,000 miles. Marriage, from this perspective, should be a relatively low-maintenance proposition if you made the right choice. Men tend to choose friends this way as well, using standards of compatibility, good feelings, common interests—and low maintenance. Most men don't fret about the state of their friendships or their marriage, unless something seems clearly wrong.

> Women, on the other hand, tend to see marriage as requiring more maintenance.

Women, on the other hand, tend to see marriage as requiring more worry and more maintenance. It is therefore common for new wives to become the primary initiators of love rituals for a couple (except for sexual contact, which men initiate more often). The husband is often happy to go along in the early years, initiating less than he used to. The result is that the leadership in the Intentional Couple shifts to one person—usually the wife—and the relationship becomes less intentional in general.[1]

And Baby Makes Three

Neither of the partners may notice much of a change in the quality of their relationship until after the birth of their first child. Now, family demands increase markedly, especially for women who usually take on the primary parenting responsibility while still being employed outside the home. Men often feel increased wage-earning pressure at this time, and may suffer from less leisure time and more responsibilities at home. A large body of research indicates that most couples experience a decline in their marital satisfaction after the birth of their first child.[2]

When new parents become focused on their baby and concomitant demands, often they put their relationship on hold. Certainly this is essential in the early weeks of having a newborn in the family, a time when just getting enough sleep is a great victory. But many couples who become highly intentional about creating good rituals of connection with their child simultaneously cease being intentional about their own relationship. The wife's leadership slackens in this regard because of her preoccupation with parenting; and the husband is out of practice at initiating couple rituals. They both settle into a low-maintenance approach to their marriage, although the wife will probably feel more regret about it. Whereas babies literally cry out for high maintenance, marriages can crank along for many years without a tune-up.

If having children tends to amplify the trend in marriage toward the Entropic Couple, can the trend be reversed? The short answer is yes. There are a number of vehicles for creating love rituals for Intentional Couples, which are described in the remainder of this chapter.

TALK TO ME

Becoming lovers involves a lot of one-to-one conversation about the ups and downs of your day, about how you are feeling, and what is important to you. Most unmarried people are incredulous when they hear their married friends say they don't have enough time to talk. What they don't yet realize is that everyday family life absorbs attention like a giant octopus, pulling and sucking first here and then there and back again. Although most couples may talk to each other on a given evening or weekend, what they lack is focused, regular time

> Few dating couples would get married if they had as little focused conversation as most married couples do.

to talk as a couple. *Most marital talk occurs in snippets rather than extended conversations.* If you are part of a couple, start paying attention to how often your conversation is lengthy enough to fill half a page of paper when written down. Few dating couples would get married if they had as little focused conversation as most married couples do.

Intentional Couples manage to create and maintain talk rituals in their everyday lives. They don't need to be time-consuming talks: 15 minutes of focused one-to-one conversation can be sufficient for couples with busy lives. But talk time *must* become a ritual or it will not happen regularly. It has to be carved out as part of the family sculpture every day.

My wife Leah and I created a talk ritual when our children were preschoolers. After the family dinner, we gave the children their dessert, cleaned up the kitchen, and started the coffee. We then sent the children off to play on their own, which they were generally willing to do at this point in the day (arsenic hour having given way to the more pleasant after-dinner period). Then we sat down at the dining room table and performed a ritual we called "having coffee," during which we talked with each other about how our days had been and anything else on our minds. Over the years, we evolved some unwritten rules for these conversations: We didn't use them to discuss conflicts or to make difficult family decisions such as how to spend money. In other words, we didn't use the time to do family "work," but rather to connect with each other at the end of the workday.

What we called "having coffee" was a true ritual, not just drinking coffee. The transition phase involved the cleanup, coffee preparation, and getting the children settled. The enactment phase too had clear norms: sitting at the dining room table; not permitting distractions such as television, newspapers, or mail; sharing "air time" during the conversation; and refraining from problem-solving. We protected this enactment phase from intrusions from the children by gently but firming steering them back to other activities, telling them this was Mom's and Dad's time to talk. Our children cannot remember a time when they were not expected to leave us alone for a while after dinner. The exit phase occurred about the time we finished our coffee, generally after about 15 minutes.

After Elizabeth, our youngest, left home for college, we began to have dinner alone as a couple for the first time in 21 years. Following an orgy of going out to eat every night for a while, we settled into having dinner at home most nights. When the meal was over, I would make coffee, pour it, and then head upstairs to do some office work. After a week or so, Leah expressed dissatisfaction with our not having coffee together any more. At first I was puzzled: We now had the entire meal for our talk time, so why did she feel the need to continue with coffee time? Then I got it: Our coffee time was a couple connection ritual on its own merits, not to be confused with having a meal together. A meal is something you have to eat in the evening, and eating it together can be just for convenience. Our coffee ritual, on the other hand, had come to represent being a loving couple. So we reinstated the ritual, and the experience was a lesson to me in the subtleties of family rituals and how easily even those well-established can be lost.

I have coached other couples on creating a daily talk ritual. Larry and Chris Murphy, the dancers, carved out 15 minutes in the morning before their child woke up. They decided not to read the paper or watch television, but just be together at this time. But Leon and Sarah Smart hated mornings and were rarely home together for dinner with their teenage daughter because Sarah taught several nights per week and didn't get home until around 8:30. With my help, Leon and Sarah negotiated the following talk ritual: When Sarah came in the door, Leon greeted her and then started water for tea while Sarah changed her clothes, chatted briefly with their daughter, and put away her work material. By the time Sarah was finished with her transition activities, the tea was ready. She and Leon sat down at the kitchen table and talked about the day, emphasizing how they were feeling rather than just reciting events or facts. I encouraged them to "take each other's emotional temperature each day." They did not problem-solve during this time, and they asked their daughter to give them privacy while they talked. (Their daughter thought they were acting strangely, but had no problem leaving them alone.) After about two months of completing this ritual intermittently, they began doing it every weeknight.

The positive effects showed up in more kindness to each other during the rest of the day, more interest in their sexual relationship, and fewer of the petty arguments that married couples have when there is no everyday connection.

Hot and Cold Talks and Walks

A couple's talk ritual should have a clear transition and a clear exit point. Ideally, the transition should be tied to some other regular event, like breakfast, dinner, or someone coming home. It is more difficult to tie the transition to a specific time, say, 9:00 P.M., because someone might be tied up with a child or on the telephone at that point. Furthermore, it should occur automatically, without negotiation each time. Thus, Leon's job was to start the tea when Sarah came home, thereby initiating the transition phase to the ritual. Similarly, the exit should be clear and non-negotiable; most couples don't have hours to spend talking each day, and it impacts the ritual if one person wants to keep talking and the other has to be the main initiator of the exit. That is why drinking something hot is helpful: You can't drink it too fast (so you have to take time to talk), but it takes a limited amount of time to drink before it's cold (so you have a clear ending point).

Some couples use walks the same way: They establish a time of the day to begin and end the walk. The problem with walks is what to do when the weather is bad; some couples don't have a substitute ritual. One couple I worked with decided to use late evening as a talk time. They join in the bedroom after the children are tucked in, and talk with each other, sitting up in bed, for at least 15 minutes. But most couples are too tired to use bedtime reliably as their talk time. In fact, the only private time most couples have is "fatigue time" at the end of the day, which does not lend itself to talk rituals.

It can be devilishly difficult to incorporate a daily 15-minute talk ritual into your life. It took Sarah and Leon a couple of months of fits and starts before incorporating it regularly into their marriage. Some couples I've worked with were not able to do it at all; their schedules were too unpredictable, or they could not discipline their children to give them the privacy. Other couples simply don't organize their lives well enough to enact a talk ritual every day: They start it, but when their schedules get in the way, they give up on the ritual. In other cases, one spouse is far more interested in the daily talk ritual than the other—a difference that dooms the arrangement.

Less Often Is More

If you are not able to incorporate a daily talk ritual, you might try to find special talk times more intermittently, such as after brunch on weekends, and then be more conscious of connecting during the routine times when you do converse every day. For example, you can try to minimize the number of times when one person is talking and the other is reading the mail or watching the television. And you can focus on some of the less frequent love rituals discussed next in this chapter. But before giving up on having daily time for private conversation, consider whether you are more diligent about talking at bedtime with your children than you are in finding a similar amount of time to talk with your spouse. Many children insist on rituals of connection with parents, whereas many spouses let their couple rituals slide. A daily talk ritual is not essential to a good marriage, but it is the surest antidote to marital entropy.

> A daily talk ritual is not essential to a good marriage, but it is the surest antidote to marital entropy.

ARE YOU FREE SATURDAY NIGHT?

My prescription for rituals of connection for couples with children include the previously discussed 15 minutes of private conversation each day, plus a "date" at least every other week.

Couples without children at home should be able to go out on dates even more frequently.

Experienced married couples often chuckle when I use the term "date," but they know what I am talking about. People who have never been married are more puzzled: Why would a couple that lives together and sleeps together every night need to go on dates? Precisely *because* they live together and sleep together. They have lots of time together, but no special time together; they are close to one another but often are not fully present to one another. That's when dates become meaningful. Dates involve getting out of the house and doing something together for the purpose of feeling—not just living—close.

The main ingredients in a marital date are privacy, enjoyment, and conversation. The activity must lend itself to all three. Going out with friends builds community but is not a date. Many married couples rarely go out alone without other couples or their own children; they have forgotten how to relate as a twosome; some even feel a bit embarrassed to sit across from each other at a nice restaurant—this same couple who at one time sought out all possible opportunities to be alone together!

Enjoyment is the second ingredient in a marital date. The activity should be pleasurable to *both* partners. It does not have to be expensive; one couple with limited income took a favorite walk along the river, followed by coffee at McDonald's. Dates fail when one or both partners cease to enjoy the outing. One wife got tired of Kung Fu movies, and her husband couldn't think of anything else he would enjoy doing on an evening out. Couples out of dating practice have trouble coming up with ideas for dates. Or each fears the other might not like the proposal; indeed, some couples avoid dates by never agreeing on what to do.

No, You Decide

In cases where there is a struggle about arranging dates, I recommend the every-other-time ritual: The couple alternates inviting the other out for a date, with the initiator proposing the time and activity at the agreed-upon interval (generally weekly or every two weeks). The invitee must agree to be open to what the other proposes, although there can be some room for negotiation. The couple then decides how they will manage baby-sitting and other logistics, preferably by sharing the workload. Alternating the leadership for dates can break a marital stalemate, when both would like to go out but neither is brave enough to make the suggestion, out of fear of the other's disinterest.

The follow-through, or lack thereof, from a partner also signals which of them has drifted farther from being intentional in the relationship. In my clinical experience, wives often follow through more faithfully than husbands in taking their turn to arrange a date. If he "forgets" on a particular week, I suggest that, for the time being, she go ahead with arranging a date when her turn comes, rather than also pulling back. And the couple needs to have frank discussion about whether they are both committed to trying this date ritual and being more intentional about their marriage.

He Said, She Said

The third ingredient in a date is having a conversation. Rushing to a movie and returning home right away does not constitute a date because it lacks concentrated time for conversation. Ditto for a bicycle outing if it does not involve breaks for quiet, calm talking together. Not that these kinds of activities are not also important for couples as connection rituals—not all connection rituals have to involve conversation—but they are not dates or love rituals because they don't allow for the possibility of intimate dialogue.

Date conversations work best when they preclude everyday problem-solving such as who is going to drive the children to camp this week, along with areas of tension and conflict in the relationship. Distressed couples are often surprised when I ask them to avoid talking about their problems during their dates. They don't realize that not only is it possible but it is valuable to put troublesome topics aside for a few hours and just enjoy each other. In fact, couples who cannot keep their conflicts from affecting their dates are more in need of help from a therapist. Date conversations should not be superficial, but they should not be work, either.

When getting back into the habit of dating, some couples feel uncomfortable during their one-to-one conversations, but this tends to pass, and, in the meantime, I suggest thinking in advance about what you might want to talk about—just as you might for a date with someone you were just getting to know.

Daniel and Lynn Campbell held onto their date ritual through some very difficult times after Lynn began to deal with the sexual abuse she had suffered as a child and subsequently felt she could not be sexual with Daniel. He felt rejected by this, and she felt guilty about hurting him. Now responsible for raising two small children, Daniel and Lynn both began wondering if they should ever have married. One of their strengths I noted in the first interview was their weekly date ritual: They had a regular baby-sitter for Saturday nights, and they always did something that was private, enjoyable, and involved time to talk. Although they had a lot of serious personal and marital work to do, this love ritual helped sustain them while they worked on their problems.

Going out for dinner has always been Leah's and my favorite date ritual. Even when we were a low-income graduate student family with two small children, we made a priority of going out to dinner every other week at a "slow food" restaurant where we would eat, drink wine, and talk. These were times to catch up with each other and to talk about the children, our families, our work, and anything else on our minds. At one restaurant in Iowa City that we frequented for a number of years, we would call ahead to reserve our favorite table that overlooked the waterfall. We would enter ritual space for a couple of hours and recharge our marital battery.

DID YOU FORGET OUR ANNIVERSARY?

Susan Abel Lieberman interviewed hundreds of families for her lovely book, *New Traditions*, on how to create new family celebrations and traditions. People were thrilled to tell her about their favorite family traditions—except for wedding anniversaries. Here is what she wrote about anniversaries:

> Anniversaries must be the least celebrated rite of passage in the nation. Most people, however cheerfully married, appear to let this occasion slide past. When I first began interviewing to collect traditions, I would ask, "What do you do for your anniversary?" Invariably, a long pause would follow. Sometimes the response was "We go out for dinner together." One lady said, "We do something together"—and then, sheepishly, "Like put in a new sewer pipe in the basement," thus aptly characterizing what lots of couples consider a reasonable anniversary celebration. It was clear that my question was making people feel embarrassed or apologetic.[3]

Lieberman's observations are in accord with my own. Most couples do not ritualize their anniversary as a special occasion. Some go out to dinner in a low-key way, although more couples celebrate their significant anniversaries—the fifth, tenth, twenty-fifth, and fiftieth—on a grander scale. But even on these occasions, it is not uncommon for couples to skip the whole thing. These same people may celebrate their and certainly their children's birthdays regularly, but when it comes to the marriage, it's all a bit embarrassing as the years go by. This is in contrast to newlyweds, who sometimes celebrate monthly anniversaries at the beginning, and then six-month anniversaries for a couple of years. Newlyweds have it right: *A wedding anniversary is the birthday of the marriage.* New parents often mark the monthly birthdays of their child for the first year, and never fail to celebrate yearly birthdays thereafter. Why be less enthused about the birthday of a marriage?

No How-To for Anniversaries

Part of the problem with anniversary rituals is that couples are pretty much on their own in figuring out what to do. For most "public" family rituals—birthdays and Christmas—there are community guidelines on how to celebrate them. You sing Happy Birthday, and you exchange Christmas gifts (if your family celebrates Christmas). And you have a cast of children driving these events. Although anniversaries are public in one sense— other people may know about it—the couple is left totally on its own to ritualize it. The only exceptions are the twenty-fifth and fiftieth anniversaries, when children sometimes orchestrate the celebration.

Left to their own devices, only Intentional Couples are likely to celebrate their anniversaries in a meaningful way after the first few years. They might take some or all of the following steps to make their anniversary a love ritual:

- *Talk about the fact that their anniversary is approaching.* Many couples let their anniversary creep up on them, one saying "Did you realize that our anniversary is next week?" Forgetting an anniversary is not uncommon, especially among husbands. When the wife believes he has forgotten and refuses to bring it up, she may be furious at him when the day arrives. It's better to mention the day well in advance.
- *Plan a special date or trip.* For a "routine" anniversary, the couple may go out on a special date, say, at their favorite restaurant. For major anniversaries, they might plan a trip together. One of the spouses can "spring" the trip on the other as a present. Either way, they plan their anniversary celebrations.
- *Remind their children and others about the anniversary.* In many families, the parents' anniversary is never discussed, and the children are not aware that it has come and gone. Making it public is a way to say the date is important.
- *Ceremonially wish each other a happy anniversary.* This may be with a special embrace in the morning, a special toast at their anniversary dinner, and special lovemaking at the beginning or end of the day. Some couples prepare brief expressions of appreciation for the other; others let an anniversary card or gift say it for them.
- *Spend some time talking about their history and future together.* Anniversaries are a wonderful time for reminiscing about the oceans of time the spouses have sailed together, and for looking ahead.

These elements in an intentionally ritualized anniversary ritual may seem impossibly structured to some, and embarrassingly intimate to others. Obviously, they are not for everybody, and there is no rule saying that you have to make your anniversary a love ritual. But any of these elements can help make your anniversary sing instead of grunt. It's going to recur every year you are married, so why not make a love ritual out of it? If it seems excessive to make a fuss over every anniversary, try this: Think back on your wedding day, and ask yourself what kind of anniversaries you would like to have in the future. Planful and joyful, or last-minute and perfunctory? My guess is that you would have voted for an intentional, ritualized anniversary every year of your marriage.

BE MY VALENTINE

Unlike anniversaries, Valentine's Day occurs on the same day for everyone. Like birthdays and other major holidays, it comes with a set of performance guidelines (card, flowers, chocolates, dinner). More married couples do something special on Valentine's Day than on their wedding anniversaries. A national poll of couples found that few admitted to doing nothing for Valentine's Day. Popular forms of celebration included: romantic dinner at a restaurant (29 percent), romantic dinner at home (11 percent), presents (30 percent), flowers (22 percent), and "something; not sure" (8 percent).[4]

Nevertheless, Valentine's Day is problematic for many married couples because the day is designed for dating couples to signal that they are each other's "sweeties." Hence, the chocolates. It is about the falling-in-love phase of an intimate relationship and not the long-term married phase. And yet Valentine's Day is a yearly occasion for spouses to show that they still have romantic feelings for each other.

Although women, too, are expected to give their husbands Valentine's gifts, the onus falls on the man to give his wife a romantic present. This probably reflects back to the traditions of courtly love in which the woman could tell the depth of her lover's feelings by the gifts he gave her. Whatever the source, the pressure is greater for the man to come through with an appropriate gift.

Couples often play unconscious games with Valentine's gifts. She may be asking indirectly, "How much do you love me?" while he is wondering, "What's your minimum expectation?" Often she won't reveal her expectations; after all, romance is supposed to be spontaneous, and thus he's supposed to read her mind. She also calibrates the quality of her gift to him by what she thinks he will give her. If she thinks he will give her a box of chocolates, she will not buy him a new bathrobe, which she might have done if she thought he would buy her a new nightgown. Meanwhile, he just wants to get through the experience without disappointing her. Given these dilemmas, many couples fall back on the standards of candy and flowers, perhaps combined with dinner at a restaurant. But even with the standards, of course, there is room for disappointment. A former student of mine was appalled when her husband bought her diet chocolates.

More personal gifts, of course, convey more personal feeling. But they can be fraught with peril, too. Spouses may give each other gifts to communicate expectations or demands, such as a husband who gives a sexy nightgown to a wife who always wears pajamas. Is he communicating disapproval of her bed attire and a wish for a racier sex life? If she wears it, is she giving in to his hidden demand or just placating him? If she does not wear it, is she rejecting him?

I confess to personal ambivalence about Valentine's Day as a marital ritual in my own life. It seems too contrived and driven by marketers of flowers and candy, and more useful for people who are declaring that they are now a couple. For me, it doesn't compare to wedding anniversaries for personal significance. But Valentine's Day is here to stay, and to ignore it is to send a message that most spouses don't want to send. My recommendation (which I intend to follow myself in the future) is to sit down with your spouse and discuss what you would like to make of Valentine's Day each year. How do you want to incorporate it into your lives? Do you want a minimal acknowledgment, perhaps a card and small box of candy or other gift? Do you want to ritualize it more significantly, say, with a special meal and a special gift? Do you want to go all out, with a romantic getaway somewhere? Instead of playing the guessing game each year, with its pressures and disappointments, couples can say to each other "Will you be my Intentional Valentine?"

The forces of entropy are powerful in marriage these days, more so than in parent-child relations, where children help us by insisting on time, attention, and rituals. Most couples begin marriage with a full tank of gas in their boat. During their early years together, they generally remember to keep refilling it, although not regularly enough or "to the top." After they have children, many couples start to run on near-empty a lot of the time, or run out of gas completely and drift toward the rocks and waterfalls. Love rituals are a renewable source of fuel to keep us afloat and heading in the direction we fondly wished for when we bravely committed ourselves to be partners for life.

Part III

FAMILY

RITUALS OF

CELEBRATION

AND COMMUNITY

SIX

Special Person Rituals: Birthdays, Mother's and Father's Day

THERE ARE SPECIAL TIMES IN FAMILIES when our personal star shines brightest in the sky, when we can revel in the love and attention of our family. That's the purpose of birthdays, Mother's Day, and Father's Day—the annual cycling of the spotlight of family life on each of its members. Historically, in the Institutional Family, families did not celebrate these days as family rituals. Until the late nineteenth century, birthdays were occasions for individual reflection, not family celebrations. Birthday rituals were the product of the new culture of individualism in Europe and America, when personal history became important, and families began to focus on individual as well as group well-being. Mother's Day and Father's Day were created in the early twentieth century amid social concern over threats to family life. Despite their recent origins, these individually focused rituals have become staples of the ritual family year, and important opportunities to celebrate connections to one another.[1]

HAPPY BIRTHDAY TO YOU

Most adults recall joyfully their birthday celebrations. It took many years for my children to even be able to distinguish between a birthday and a birthday party, since the party loomed so large in their consciousness. From age 2 onward, there is no more personalized big event for children than their annual birthday ritual. As children, we see these events as the beginning of many birthdays to come. When we're older, we reflect on our long journey and wonder how many more miles we have left to walk. In between, birthdays mark rites of passage: to the teen years, to driving age, to legal adulthood, to perhaps parenthood. Intentional Families thus use birthday rituals to celebrate a life, to reminisce, and to hope.

Although every cultural group has its own spin on children's birthdays, certain elements are traditional in mainstream America: the cake, the candles, the singing of "Happy Birthday," the birthday person blowing out the candles and opening presents. Other elements are optional, such as who is in attendance and whether to have the party at home or at a restaurant. There is a lot of room to be creative and intentional about birthdays.

Not So Happy Birthdays

Skipping a child's birthday generally is not an option. There is tremendous pressure on families to arrange a birthday celebration for every child each year. Neglecting birthday acknowledgments is regarded as a serious breach of parental responsibility in our culture. Pam Wiegert described how, after her mother died, her father often forgot to arrange birthday parties for his three children. Decades later, Pam's face revealed her ongoing pain as she told the story of a father so overwhelmed with raising children that he skipped the "extras." He fed and clothed them, but he failed to celebrate his children's special days. Those birthdays can never be retrieved. Significantly, Pam makes birthdays special in her own family.

Even when birthday rituals are enacted, however, they can be empty. Rosalie Cowan hated arranging birthday parties for her two small children, and she admitted as much when she called other parents to invite her children's friends. Her own childhood birthday parties were scenes of sibling fights and parental apathy, a tradition she unfortunately continued with her own children. It didn't help that Rosalie was a single parent with too much work to do at home and on the job. And because Rosalie was a fairly disorganized person, arranging a party was a major headache. Each time she thought she had all the party paraphernalia together, she would realize she forgot something and have to return to the store. Nor did she have good skills in managing children's behavior. She expected an out-of-control party each year, and that's what she got. Rosalie hovered around barking orders until the last child went home, done for another year.

To her credit, Rosalie never failed to give her children birthday parties, even though she dreaded them. What could she have done to make birthday rituals more intentional and more satisfying? For one thing, she could have had a smaller, quieter party with just herself and her children—and skip having eight 5-year-olds in her house. If she wanted to have her children's friends over, she could invite other parents, a relative, and a friend to help handle the child management issues while she concentrated on the ritual. She also could plan organized activities for the children. If she had the money, she could reserve space at a local fast-food restaurant for the party, and invite the other children's parents to stay for the party. What she did right was to have the party, despite her feelings; her mistake was to make it a hollow ritual.

But well-done birthday rituals, too, have their pitfalls. For young children especially, attending another child's party, especially one for a sibling, can create feelings of envy. That's the downside of the focus on one individual: the spotlight is off the others. Children naturally will compare their own parties and presents with those of their siblings and friends. One friend's daughter only wanted to give presents that she already had herself, maintaining that "I get jealous if it's something I can't have."

To head off these sibling and peer issues, and to make each child in attendance feel special, my wife Leah always gave a small token present to the other children attending the birthday party. (Since our own children's birthdays were in June and December, we also acknowledged the half-birthday of the other child.) Every child left with a treat. This was not part of my childhood birthday rituals, but I was impressed with how this simple act of providing for everyone enhanced our children's birthday celebrations. It reminded me of an American Indian ritual I witnessed, in which the winner of the dancing competition gave gifts to the other competitors.

One family told me that they symbolize *both* the birthday person and the family by lighting a large candle for the birthday person and surrounding it with smaller candles for the other members of the family. Then everyone blows out their candle at the same time.

HOW OLD ARE YOU NOW?

Although childhood birthday rituals are important in most American families, adult birthdays are another matter. While in some families, they are a big deal, as important as children's birthdays, in other families, adult birthdays, especially those of the parents, are neither acknowledged nor celebrated.

As a child, Marcia Simpson's birthday was so important in her family that she grew up thinking it was a national holiday. Her parents always kept her home from school on her birthday and did something special with her. As an adult, she continued to feel the same way about her birthdays, that there was no bigger personal event in the year. And she treated other people's birthdays the same way. Naturally, Marcia married Jim, whose family stopped celebrating their children's birthdays after they reached age 21.

During the two years of their courtship, Marcia's and Jim's family differences on birthdays were merely a source of bemused discussion. Marcia could not fathom Jim's family's neglect of its adult members. Jim tried to explain that a card on his birthday was enough; when he was growing up, he didn't even know when his parents' birthdays were. (To this day, he has trouble remembering them.) To him, birthday rituals were for children— like going out on Halloween.

Marcia thought this custom strange and a bit disturbing, but felt confident it would not impact her new family, because during their courtship, Jim made a big deal of her birthday, as he did Valentine's Day, the anniversary of their first meeting, and other sentimental occasions. But as their newlywed years turned into parenting years and they began to celebrate their children's birthdays, Jim did less and less for Marcia's birthday each year. It wasn't a conscious decision, just the way he had learned that parents relate to each other. Special occasions were for the children.

As you can imagine, Marcia was not happy with this change. Each year she had to struggle with being grateful for the way Jim acknowledged her birthday (presents and a small party), but she really felt hurt and angry that her birthday had declined from national holiday status to something fairly routine. When she complained, Jim felt unappreciated and upset with Marcia for being so hard to please. As their annual struggles recurred, he came to see her as self-centered and even selfish about her birthdays; after all, he did not expect such a fuss for his birthday, nor did his family or friends. Marcia came to see Jim as less caring and sensitive than he was when they first married.

Otherwise, Marcia and Jim had a good marriage. They enacted most other family rituals without conflict, although like most couples, they were not intentional about their couple rituals. But the disparity on the adult birthday issue unfortunately became a drain on their marital battery. As time went on, they had fewer reserves when they needed them, say, during a serious marital conflict or when one of them was exceptionally busy with work. They became less able to resist the forces of entropy in their relationship.

IT'S YOUR PARTY

How can couples turn birthdays into a plus rather than a minus? For starters, they will have to stop arguing over whose family "knows" the right way to handle adult birthdays. There is no rule book. Marcia's family may place far more emphasis on birthdays than Jim's does, but in both families, people feel loved and cared for. Jim's family has other rituals it emphasizes more than Marcia's, such as family camping and biking trips. The first step toward resolving differences is to accept them, to stop labeling others and their families with terms such as "insensitive" and "selfish."

The next step is to become more intentional as a couple about birthday rituals. In Jim's and Marcia's case, rather than hoping Jim will figure out what she wants, Marcia should spell out the elements of the kind of birthday celebration that make her happy. These might include a party with their children, a bigger party with extended family and close friends, several nice gifts from Jim, lunch during the day at their favorite spot, and a call to her colleagues at work reminding them of her birthday. Jim can either agree to do these things for her each year, or ask her to share some of the responsibilities, such as in planning for a bigger party. Further, he should agree to do them not because he "agrees" that this is how adults should celebrate birthdays, but because he loves Marcia and wants her to have a happy birthday. Similarly, Jim should tell Marcia what he would like for his birthday ritual, which, of course, will probably be less involved than Marcia's.

> We must be particularly intentional about rituals such as adult birthdays that have such different meanings for people. Sometimes the Golden Rule needs a twist: Do not for others what you would have them do for you—find out first what they want.

A similar situation occurs when intimates are sick. Some people want to be pampered, showered with frequent expressions of sympathy and offers of assistance. They like lots of TLC; the more the better. Other people just want to be left alone—the "I'll let you know if I need something" type. Unfortunately, the two types often marry each other, with predictable results: The partner who wants lots of nurturing when sick feels neglected and abandoned, while the other is annoyed by the dependency and demands. The solution, easy to say but difficult to do, is to give the others what they want, and not what *we* would want in the same situation. This is possible only if we take a nonblaming approach to a discussion about our preferences, and come to a clear agreement about what we can expect of each other.

We must be particularly intentional about rituals such as adult birthdays that have such different meanings for people. Sometimes the Golden Rule needs a twist: Do not for others what you would have them do for you—find out first what they want.

Still Going After All These Years

My father-in-law's 80th birthday celebration was a community affair. My wife and her siblings rented the town hall, sent out invitations, and put an invitation in the local newspaper (a common occurrence in small towns). Over a hundred people showed up in a ritual that brought together all the ships still afloat in this man's life convoy: his wife, children, grandchildren, and long-term friends, and neighbors. His own siblings were all dead.

My in-laws greeted the guests as they entered the hall. Some they had seen that day, and others not for months or years. The children and older grandchildren hustled about getting people food and beverages. You never know how many people will show up at these events—RSVP's are not the custom—and you hope you have enough food. Somehow you always do.

This gathering of people important to my father-in-law, along with the traditional birthday song and candles, alone would have made it a special birthday. But it was the extras that made it memorable. My wife Leah, the oldest child, gave a moving welcome, saying how glad the family was to have them there to celebrate this important birthday. Then she asked people to introduce themselves and say something about their connection to her father. A lifetime of memories poured forth, from high-school classmates to neighbors so close they felt like kin. In this ritual setting, people felt comfortable saying things they would not otherwise share. My heart was full as I taped each statement with a camcorder. We gave my father-in-law a copy of the tape, which he watched over and over.

When my mother celebrated her 80th birthday along with her twin sister, they were surrounded by several generations of relatives and a few close friends of the family. As I called the group to silence before the formal birthday ritual began, my mother could sense that I was going to make a special toast, and she began to cry. What I witnessed next was a scene that no doubt had been repeated often over 80 years although I had never before been privy to it: twin sisters, now both widowed, one comforting the other and stroking her hair. My toast was not particularly memorable—something about how happy and fortunate we were to have these two sisters be our mothers for so many years. What was memorable was how moved my mother was that I would say something personal at her party, and that she and her sister demonstrated publicly how they had comforted each other during their life together. Family rituals can fill our hearts and give us lifetime memories.

INTENTIONAL AND INTIMATE BIRTHDAY RITUALS

There are innumerable ways to be intentional about birthday rituals: gifts, party locations and fanfare, dining at special restaurants, taking special trips, and so forth. But especially enriching is the sharing of personal appreciations.

In the last two years, my family has instituted an appreciation ritual for birthdays and other special occasions. After the Happy Birthday song is sung and the candles are blown out, and while we are eating cake and ice cream, we take turns telling the birthday person what we value and appreciate about him or her, perhaps something we especially noticed in the past year. The ritual can be quite revealing and moving. I told my son Eric, on his 23rd birthday, how proud I was of his transition from college to independent adulthood in the past year. I told my daughter Elizabeth how much I admired her courage in planning a trip to Europe at age 20, something I would have been terrified to do. And I told my wife Leah how much I admired her loving commitment to her parents, who that year had to move to a nursing home. Probably my family knew I had these thoughts and feelings about them, but there is great power in the ritualized telling. These emotional gifts linger longer in memory than any tangible gift.

Ritual Growth

New rituals can be fragile until their roots become strong over time and with repetition. Because Leah and I were out of town for Eric's birthday this past year and his sister Elizabeth was out of the country, we had a makeshift birthday party, with just the three of us, a couple of weeks after the actual date, and we forgot to do our new ritual of appreciation. When we celebrated Leah's birthday a few weeks later, we almost overlooked it again, but Eric reminded us, and said that he had missed his turn. So we did the appreciation ritual first for him and then for his mother. This incident helps make two points: Even very rewarding new rituals can easily fall prey to entropy, and it helps when all family members are willing to take leadership in calling the family back to its rituals.

> Even very rewarding new rituals can easily fall prey to entropy, and it helps when all family members are willing to take leadership in calling the family back to its rituals.

I recommend adding a personal appreciation ritual to your birthday celebrations. If you begin when the children are young, they will come to love and expect it. But this ritual can be implemented with adolescents or with adult children as well, or between a couple. People should feel free to share whatever comes to their mind; it can be something "deep" or more superficial, as long as the appreciation is genuine. The first year, a teenager might say to his parents, "I appreciate your letting me drive the family car this year." A few years later, he might say how much he appreciates the kind of father his dad has been. In the last chapter of this book, I will share strategies for getting started with rituals such as this.

MOTHER'S DAY

We wouldn't have Mother's Day if everything were fine with motherhood. (The same is true for Father's Day.) Social historians tell us that the movement for Mother's Day arose out of concern for family life and parenting at the turn of the twentieth century. During the nineteenth century, the principal task of mothers was childrearing, with fathers expected to support the family outside the home. As the Institutional Family quickened its disintegration a century ago, many people were worried about whether American families could continue to do a good job of raising children. Mothers were under increasing pressure to work in factories, and community and extended family support for raising children was being depleted. Since mothers were seen as the bastions of family life, many people saw the need for a day to acknowledge their importance. Florists and greeting card manufacturers, for more capitalistic reasons, loved the idea and became principal promoters of creating a national Mother's Day, which became official in 1909.[2]

It took awhile for Mother's Day to move from a public pronouncement to a routine family ritual. Families had to figure out what to make of it. Over the years, a few social norms have evolved: give a card, flowers, or a present; and perhaps "treat" Mom by taking her out for a meal. Adult children living away from home are expected to telephone their mother, making Mother's Day the busiest long-distance call day of the year. Not doing so usually signals a serious breach.

Who's in Charge

The main challenge on Mother's Day is who is going to take responsibility for the ritual, because in most families the mother gen-

erally orchestrates the family's rituals. Furthermore, there may be four or more mothers in the same family who need attention: two grandmothers, great-grandmothers, and a mother. A mother in a particular family may be generating a ritual celebration for her and/or her husband's mother, while at the same time hoping that her husband or children do the same for her. All of the celebrations can folded into one, with one of the mothers in control, although that person may feel angry and resentful and overlooked.[3]

This dilemma on Mother's Day points to the issue of men's roles in family rituals. Many men remain passive about family rituals throughout their lives, leaving leadership to their mothers, wives, and sisters. Women, for their part, grow up expecting men to absent themselves from planning and otherwise taking the lead in family rituals. They expect men to "help out" rather than be intentional.

If the women in the family are good at family rituals, and if they enjoy the responsibility and get enough help from men and children, then the family may have a rich ritualizing life without much leadership from the husbands, fathers, brothers, and sons. But when the ritual focuses on the mother—birthdays and Mother's Day—a major hole in the family ritual can develop, followed by major disappointment and hurt feelings.

After men marry, they commonly expect their wives to manage cards and gifts for both mothers on Mother's Day. While this works for some couples, others struggle over what to do for the husband's mother. Brenda and Larry Cummings fought every year around Mother's Day because he did not want to plan anything special for his mother, other than perhaps promise to call her. Brenda, who went to greater lengths for her own mother, felt guilty that Larry and she did not do anything special for his mother. Larry couldn't understand why Brenda was upset at how he treated his own mother. In his family, he protested, Mother's Day was never important.

What Larry didn't realize was how Brenda was implicated in his minimalist approach to Mother's Day. First, Brenda liked her mother-in-law and wanted to do something for her; second, Brenda had good reason to believe that her mother-in-law held

Brenda partly responsible for the low-effort ritual every year. I learned from Larry that he did not have a problem with honoring his mother on Mother's Day; he just didn't want to be pressured by his wife to do anything other than phone her. When I inquired whether he minded if Brenda did what she wanted for his mother, he said no. Following this discussion, Brenda was free to buy her mother-in-law a card or flowers if she liked, while refraining from pressuring Larry about what he should do.

This illustrates the complexities of male-female dynamics in family rituals. Women often handle the events unless only the man is in the position to take the lead. At this point, their different expectations for rituals become a source of distress. On Mother's Day, it is particularly tricky for the mother herself. If her husband does not take an active role, but she has a daughter, a mother can expect at some point that her daughter will become active in managing Mother's Day (and mother's birthday). Many husbands and fathers, unprepared to be family ritualizers, are happy to have the help from their teenage and adult daughters. The bottom line is, men have to get on board if a family is to be truly intentional. In the last chapter, we will discuss how men can change their involvement in family rituals.

FATHER'S DAY

I often receive requests to be interviewed as Father's Day approaches each year. Sadly, fathers are often portrayed in our culture and in the media as absent, "deadbeat," and abusive. Indeed, there are numbers to support these stereotypes: about 40 percent of children do not live with their father; many nonresidential fathers do not pay full child support; and too many fathers are neglectful or abusive in the home.[4] And because so many children have such conflicted relationships with their fathers, especially nonresidential fathers, Father's Day no doubt brings more pain to children than does Mother's Day.

Father's Day became a national celebration for many of the same reasons as Mother's Day: a concern about the meaning of

fatherhood in the early twentieth century. There was more oppo-
sition to this holiday, however, from public figures who thought
that celebrating fathers might undermine mothers' preeminence
in childrearing. Once again, though, commercial interests such
as department stores and haberdasheries got on the bandwagon.
Nevertheless, it was not until 1969 that Father's Day was given
national recognition by means of a presidential decree. By then,
there was even greater national concern about the role of fathers
in family life.[5]

There are fewer social norms for Father's Day than for Mother's
Day: a card, a phone call, or a gift is all that's expected. The main
requirement is some contact and acknowledgment. Celebrating
Father's Day is also less dicey in most families because the mother
fills her routine role of organizing the children and orchestrating
the ritual. The wife probably also handles her husband's acknowledgment of his own father. Things tend to go smoothly when the
father lives in the same home with his children.

When the father lives elsewhere, the mother has to decide how
to deal with Father's Day. If the child has an ongoing relationship with his or her father, then the mother will probably help
the child buy a Father's Day card or make a present, and either
call the father or make arrangements for the child to see him. If
the child has no relationship, then the mother is likely to hold
back and hope that the day is not too painful. (I discuss in Chapter Eleven some ways to make family rituals such as Father's
Day meaningful in single-parent families.)

A Step in the Right Direction

Acknowledging stepfathers on Father's Day can be more difficult. Children are often torn about their stepparents: If they
bond too closely to the stepparent, they may feel disloyal to their
original parent. (I say "original" because it can be either a biological or adoptive parent.) And because more children live with
stepfathers than with stepmothers, I recommend that mothers
allow their children to determine themselves how much they

want to do for their stepfather on Father's Day. In the early years, they may do nothing, and then later give a card, and later still something more personal. The stepparent/stepchild relationship has to be allowed to mature at its own pace over time. And when children want to celebrate a stepfather (or stepmother), it's a happy moment for all.

Whether celebrating Father's Day or Mother's Day, one way to be intentional and personal is to conduct a ritual of sharing appreciations similar to the one I described for birthdays. To try this, let the spotlight shine for a few minutes on Dad or Mom by inviting each family member to offer a few words of acknowledgment, gratitude, and appreciation. The ritual could take the form of a series of toasts, and the words can be simple and brief, or lengthy and emotional. The parent-child bond has the most powerful emotional resonance in the human experience. A ritual of appreciation helps to put words to that resonance at least once a year.

Thanksgiving

M ARGE BAUGHMAN AND HER HUSBAND PETE have successfully created Intentional Family rituals with their 3-year-old son Seth for family dinners, birthdays, bedtimes—everything, that is, except Thanksgiving, when Marge relinquishes control of her family rituals to her mother-in-law Lydia, who runs Thanksgiving with a benevolent, but iron, hand. The mother of four grown children, Lydia insists that all Thanksgiving celebrations be at her house—and that she do all the work herself. The result is that Marge never has Thanksgiving with her own parents, who also live nearby, and she never gets the chance to host the meal at her own house. She has given up her family of origin's Thanksgiving rituals and cannot start her own.

When one year Marge tried to beg off Thanksgiving at Lydia's by asserting that she wanted to celebrate with her own family, Lydia told Marge to invite *her* family to join *them*. "It wouldn't be Thanksgiving without all my children and grandchildren," Lydia declared, "and of course all my children's in-laws are most welcome." Marge's family was not interested, thank you.

Family therapists like to say it really takes three to tango, not two. The key third party here, of course, is Pete, who brushes off Marge's complaints about his mother's behavior. "It's a big deal to her," Pete would say, "and we all have a good time." And he thinks his mother's suggestion that Marge's family come to Lydia's house is a great compromise. Pete is not *opposed* to visiting Marge's parents for the Thanksgiving meal, but he will not suggest it to his mother.

Thanksgiving occupies a unique place in American family rituals, which is why families like the Baughmans struggle over it. Marge's family is Jewish and Pete's is Christian, so Christmas does not present a problem. But Thanksgiving is important to Marge, as it is to almost all Americans who are not recent immigrants. Thanksgiving is a nonsectarian holiday whose defining characteristic is a meal with the extended family. It is celebrated by all Americans, as opposed to a sectarian religious holiday like Christmas, which many non-Christians do not celebrate. Thus, at Thanksgiving as at no other time in the year, families often compete for the right to maintain their annual ritual celebration.

Thanksgiving is our one true national family holiday. Its origins have little to do with the Pilgrims, who celebrated the thanksgiving feast for only a couple of years. Actually, periodic days of thanks to the gods for a good harvest harken back to ancient Roman and Greek times. During European history, leaders occasionally declared special days of gratitude to God for victories in battle. In early American history, George Washington and other presidents declared days of special thanks for events such as the adoption of the Constitution and victory in the War of 1812. Thanksgiving as a fixed annual holiday in this country was an idea that grew during the first half of the nineteenth century, spearheaded by Sarah Josepha Hale, the editor of the women's magazine *Godey's Lady's Book*. For 40 consecutive years, Hale wrote editorials and letters to the presidents calling for an annual day of giving thanks. Her goal was to promote national unity during an era when tensions between North and South were threatening the Union. In 1863, after the Battle of Gettysburg, Abraham Lincoln issued a proclamation that the last Thursday in November would be an annual day of thanksgiving. Debates occurred among the states over the next 80 years about the proper date in November to hold Thanksgiving; it was not until 1941 that Congress deemed the fourth Thursday of November as Thanksgiving. Whereas earlier generations of Americans emphasized public celebrations and religious services, in our time, Thanksgiving has become a ritual for families; to celebrate it, millions of Americans flock home every year.[1]

culean efforts. (Hercules, remember, did not ask for an assist when he tore down the pillars of the pagan temple.)

Teamwork

In addition to the burden on the host, the problem with one person doing all the Thanksgiving work is that it violates one of the canons of good family rituals: maximum participation. Sharing the preparation and cleanup engages people in the ritual more meaningfully than just showing up and eating. Certainly, the host can cook the turkey, which is the centerpiece, but sharing the rest of the food preparation adds to the group's enjoyment of Thanksgiving.

It need not be said that in most American families, women do most of the food preparation for Thanksgiving. Men have learned to be passive recipients of the bounty. The male host's role often is confined to carving the turkey, which itself is becoming a lost art to the current generation of men.[4] This unequal division of ritual labor is not good for Thanksgiving, and it is not good for couples. Cooking skill is not the issue here, although some men and women use it as the reason they do not share the workload. Even if he can't boil an egg, a man can serve as a house preparer and assistant chef—if the woman is willing to share the responsibility and some of the glory, and if he is willing to be a partner. And many men have good culinary skills if they and their wives are willing to use them.

> In addition to the burden on the host, the problem with one person doing all the Thanksgiving work is that it violates one of the canons of good family rituals: maximum participation.

Rosie and Don had their entire clan over every year for a Thanksgiving dinner that was a low point for them as a couple. Rosie complained that she never got to interact with anyone during the day because she was working alone in the kitchen. Don played the gracious host, refilling drinks and orchestrating board games. Rosie would periodically call him into the kitchen to do something for her, after which he returned to the guests. As the day wore on, she would grow more irritable about her requests for help, and he would avoid passing through the kitchen. She felt abandoned, and he felt criticized for not anticipating that she would want him for something. After we discussed this pattern in marital therapy, Rosie realized that what she wanted was for Don to stay with her for blocks of time to assist; but more than that, she wanted him there as her partner. Having to call him away from the guests made her feel unsupported and him feel imposed upon. Don realized that Rosie needed his active presence in the kitchen, not just his response when she called. So he decided to camp out in the kitchen with her for periods of time to participate in the food preparation and to simply talk with her about how it was going. The guests did quite well on their own, and both Rosie and Don had something additional to be thankful for that year—a new sense of partnership in family rituals.

What about the rest of the family, especially those who shirk any labor on Thanksgiving? One way to increase involvement is to orchestrate the cleanup. As with all important shifts in family rituals, it's best to prepare people in advance. In one family, the hosts decided on their strategy before Thanksgiving Day. At a prearranged time, just after the food was served and everyone gave hearty congratulations to the main chef, the husband announced that this year the guys were going to handle the cleanup, and the women were going to relax after the meal. Who could seriously object? Then the husband made sure no one slipped away afterward. The men and teenage boys had a good time talking and cleaning in the kitchen, and sometimes had to steer away the women who tried to help. Once the precedent was set, it was easy to continue this part of the ritual on subsequent Thanksgivings.

In another family, the hostess has everyone draw a job from a hat. No one objects and everyone participates. Compare these examples to the following more common way that people try to bring about change in family rituals: Mom is exhausted and fretful about something gone awry with the meal. The other women have been scurrying about trying to set the table and get the food on the table, plus corral the children. The men have been watching football and asking when dinner is. When every-one is finished eating and feeling pleasantly full, one of the adult daughters blurts out:"Why don't the men clean up for a change? It wouldn't kill any of you to help out a little." This kind of out-burst produces waves of defensiveness on the part of the men, plus a rescue attempt from Mom who says that she will handle the cleanup herself. The ritual ends on a sour note. Some of the men who may have been planning to help are angry at being scolded, while others go through a few perfunctory cleaning motions, then head for the television. And the women clean up once more. Happy Thanksgiving.

The intentional approach to changing the logistics of family rituals encourages a shift without souring the ritual itself. The key is advance planning and low-key but firm proposals made by the right person at the right time. For Rosie and Don, it meant understanding the importance of being ritual partners instead of having an isolated boss and a fetch-it underling. In the case of the cleanup operation, the key was that the husband called on the other men to pitch in and then took the lead in the kitchen.

WARMING UP AND COOLING DOWN

The transition phase of the Thanksgiving family ritual is often unsatisfying. The meal planners are busy with their work, but no one else has anything to do. This is especially difficult for chil-dren, who may be cooped up with their siblings and cousins, perhaps in their good clothes. There are too many adult super-visors around, and rivals messing with their toys. Then, too, the big meal may be served at an unusual time, such as 2:00 P.M. This throws children's (and adults') eating schedules off; they may have been deprived of a real lunch. And although there may be lots of goodies available, parents order them not to eat too much or they will spoil their dinner. The family barometric pressure rises steadily. Will the turkey be done on time? How long before grandpa gets fed up with the children's noise? Soon a minor argument breaks out between two children, and three adults respond too strongly. Great day so far.

Following the meal usually is less tense, but may have its own problems. People are overfed, as etiquette requires; they are lethargic. The children are restless from sitting politely at the table for longer than usual. The Thanksgiving ritual is over. Now what? The rest of the afternoon can be one of the more boring times of the year. Football helps for some; naps for others. The host is ready to collapse but feels responsible for everyone's good time. No one can go home yet, because it would be unseemly to leave so soon.

If any of this sounds familiar, then why not instigate new Thanksgiving activities for before *and* after the meal? We highly ritualize what is served at the meal but underritualize the rest of the day. Pre-mealtime cannot be organized for everyone, since some family members will be involved in food preparation, but activities can be organized for the children and perhaps for the adults. One simple suggestion is to plug a video into the VCR for the children. If there are children of different ages, and more than one TV available, ask a relative to bring another VCR, and show two movies simultaneously. If the weather is nice, organize outside games for the children and adults. And quiet age-appropriate inside games are always in order. Just don't plan nothing; free-form children's play is not apt to work well in a house crammed with guests.

Adults too can benefit from being invited to participate in planned activities before and after the meal. Board or card games can be set up, as well as video options that adults might like. One year, my family watched the entire three episodes of the *Star Wars* trilogy before and after the meal. It brought back warm memories for our adult children, who remembered *Star Wars* as the first great movie event of their early years. We discussed the movies from an adult perspective as we watched together. A standard post-Thanksgiving activity my family enjoys when we celebrate at our house is to visit the Como Park Conservatory in St. Paul, where we walk among the tropical plants and flowers on a cold Minnesota afternoon. Getting outside, piling into a few cars, and walking amidst the natural beauty puts everyone in a good mood and gets them hungry enough for the leftovers that usher in the end of the Thanksgiving Day ritual. Whatever your family chooses to do before and after the main meal, it can be helpful to plan in advance and offer a number of options to keep people engaged and connected—in other words, to be intentional about the whole day.

GRACEFUL ENTRANCE

The Baptist theologian Harvey Cox said that "Excess is at the heart of festivity." Excess and Thanksgiving are nearly synonymous in our culture. We set out the large dinner plates and plenty of side plates to accommodate the cornucopia of food. It takes 10 minutes before everyone piles something from every dish onto their plate, and if you are seated in the middle of the table, you can spend half your time passing food. Everyone moans about the excess—and loves it.

The cook is expected to be openly humble about the food; she (or he) even apologizes for one or two dishes, or asks if they are okay. "The turkey is too dry," she says. To which the guests reply in chorus: "The turkey tastes just fine." The cook, or the cook's spouse, continually exhorts people to have more helpings. Usually, one item is forgotten, such as buns in the oven or the creamed corn. With profuse apologies, the item is retrieved, while everyone else dutifully claims it was not missed.

These are typical elements in the Thanksgiving meal conversation. In some families, there may also be a prayer before the meal, which can be uncomfortable for guests who do not pray before dinner during the rest of the year. And when done in a rote fashion, the Thanksgiving prayer is usually not very meaningful. With thought and preparation, however, when the family has a tradition of offering prayers of thanks at meals, they can be a meaningful way to mark the transition to the ritual meal.

Bottoms Up

The rest of the Thanksgiving meal and conversation generally is a free-for-all, which for some families is enjoyable and for others a source of tension. The Zinn family's Thanksgiving meals have been marred for years by Uncle Otto's drinking. Otto gets drunk on the wine every Thanksgiving, and embarrasses everyone. Gentle reminders about not having another glass of wine are lost on him, as are serious discussions over the years about getting help.

Otto's niece Diane consulted me about how to handle this delicate situation at her house, which was to be the site for the second year in a row. She did not want a repeat of the previous year when Uncle Otto fell headlong into his turkey dressing. But neither did Diane want to offend Otto by excluding him from the celebration. What's more, his sister, Diane's mother, would not brook her baby brother being alone on Thanksgiving. So not inviting Otto was not an option; he was family. Telling him in advance not to drink too much was pointless since Otto didn't think he drank too much last year (he was just sleepy, he said). Diane considered not serving wine with the meal, but felt that would deprive everyone else of something that made this meal special. And people might assume she forgot it, and rush home to get some.

I asked Diane how much wine she had on hand last year. As you can imagine, she had plenty; who wants to run out of anything on Thanksgiving? Wine was available before the meal, when Uncle Otto would get his head start, and in abundant supply during the meal. I asked the obvious question: "Why not limit the amount of wine available?" That shift worked well for Diane. She bought far less wine this year and kept it squirreled away before the meal, leaving only soft drinks out in the open. When Otto asked where the wine was, she replied that she was saving it for the meal. During the meal, she poured a glass for each adult who drank wine, leaving a little less than a half-bottle on the table for refills. Otto could manage only one refill. And no one asked whether there was more wine, since this was a breach of Thanksgiving etiquette. Uncle Otto stayed awake and charming throughout the meal.

This adjustment helped everyone, including Uncle Otto, to better enjoy the Thanksgiving meal. It was carried out without angry words or embarrassment to anyone. Uncle Otto does have a drinking problem, but Thanksgiving at his niece's house was not the time for the family to deal with it. Instead, Diane helped the family to maintain the integrity of its annual Thanksgiving ritual by circumventing a predictable pattern that undermined the ritual. Researchers at George Washington University have documented the positive effects on future generations when families maintain their family rituals in the face of alcoholism.[5]

For What We Are About to Receive

In addition to being intentional about preventing family disruptions during the Thanksgiving meal, there are proactive ways to enhance the meaning of the celebration. One way is to ritualize the giving of thanks. In the Jackson family, Ken Jackson takes seriously his responsibility to formulate a family prayer of thanksgiving each year. After he finishes, everyone is invited to say what they are thankful for in the past year. When Ken Jackson determines that all who want to have spoken, he says, simply, "Amen. Let's eat."

The Jackson's giving of thanks could be enhanced by involving more family members and ritualizing it even more. The problem with a free-form sharing of thanks is that people don't know who else is going to participate, who is going to go next, and when the sharing is finished. People sometimes speak up at the same time, the children either hold back or take over, and there are long pauses. A small ritual enhancement could go like this: After Ken Jackson's prayer, he could invite everyone to share something they are thankful for this year, beginning with the youngest family member who is able to participate to the oldest. If the family does not say formal prayers, the host can simply invite the sharing of thanks, in order of age, and take his or her turn at the appropriate time.

A sharing ritual like this works best when each family member makes one brief comment, such as "I give thanks that Mom has recovered so well from her surgery," or "I give thanks for not losing my job this year." Small children are expert at brief expressions of thanks, such as for their dog. Don't let the food get cold while people give speeches. Speaking in age order also calls forth something deep and important about generations in families. When a family conducts this ritual of sharing thanks each year, people prepare themselves and their children ahead of time, which reduces the pressure about what to say.

If the conversation and sharing during Thanksgiving already work well for you, then just let it flow. If you want to enhance the "thanks" element in the ritual, try an organized approach to giving people the opportunity to express their gratitude. Warning: Read Chapter 12 before you unilaterally impose a sharing ritual into your Thanksgiving meal. Family traditions don't change smoothly without a well thought-out plan of action, consultation, and persuasion.

THANKS FOR THANKSGIVING

If we have just one universal family ritual celebration each year, I'm glad it is Thanksgiving, because it has not been as highly commercialized as many others. You don't have to spend a lot of money for Thanksgiving gifts, cards, and wrapping paper. Aside from a few cardboard turkeys, your sensibilities are not assaulted every time you enter a mall. Walter Shapiro, a *Time* magazine columnist, wrote in an essay titled "Why We've Failed to Ruin Thanksgiving":

> Americans have grown inured to crass commercialism taken to
> excess. . . . But somehow Thanksgiving has resisted the blandish-
> ments of an age of avarice. . . . In a nation where the mall never
> palls and seven-days-a-week shopping seems enshrined as a civic

religion, Thanksgiving stands out as an oasis of tranquillity and a reminder of the values that once tempered American materialism. This Thursday give thanks for the one holiday that cannot be bought.[6]

Thanksgiving may have started nearly 150 years ago as a day of national unity, but it has been transformed by millions of Americans into a day of family unity, a day for connection across generations and space and time, and a day for religious feeling that crosses sectarian lines. When we can't be with our extended family at Thanksgiving, most of us call them. Contact is the thing, although preferably face to face. Being with Uncle Otto somehow becomes significant, drinking problem and all.

One Thanksgiving a few years ago, I learned that not even the turkey is very important. We were to spend Thanksgiving Day with Leah's family in Iowa, a five- to six-hour drive away. Her mother's failing health meant she could not cook the Thanksgiving meal for the clan, and so the family decided to dine at the local community restaurant. But a snowstorm delayed our leavetaking until Thursday morning, when we headed for Iowa, taking the long route to avoid the worst roads.

It was past 1:00 P.M. by the time we arrived, and past 1:30 P.M. by the time the whole group made it to the restaurant, which was by then out of turkey. Instead, they offered us fried chicken—on the house. It was a memorable Thanksgiving meal nonetheless because we all cared enough to be together despite health problems and winter.

Minnesota writer and radio host Garrison Keillor penned the following reflections about Thanksgiving, which his family celebrated at Uncle Don's and Aunt Elsie's in south Minneapolis each year. Comparing Thanksgiving with the complexity of Christmas and its requirement for tasteful gifts, he wrote:

Thanksgiving is a peasant holiday, and good taste has never been part of it. That's why it is such a comfort. All you have to do is sit down. . . . After my aunt died last fall I bought her dining-room table from my uncle, who went south; and now it will hold my dinner, which is like hers and almost as good. Thanksgiving isn't hard to make, which is the beauty of it. You fix a big table full of dinner and plop down and think, life is good, thank you for this, it could be a lot worse, and I'm grateful it's not. God bless us. More we do not need.[7]

CHAPTER

EIGHT

Christmas

Like most people, i never knew any other way to celebrate Christmas than my family's until I got married. Some couples argue over what kind of tree to buy (natural or artificial, tall and scraggly, or short and bushy) and when to put it up. Fortunately, both my wife's and my family "do" their trees in the "right" way: Buy a tall, scraggly tree and put it up and decorate it on Christmas Eve.

Our difference was over how to decorate the tree. On Christmas Eve 1971, I discovered that I came from a family of tinsel "throwers" (creatively flinging handsful of tinsel at the tree) and that my wife came from a family of tinsel "placers" (fastidiously draping each strand over its appointed branch). "What are you doing?" my wife asked in horror as she entered the room and witnessed her new husband standing on a ladder and hurling tinsel at the tree. An extended discussion ensued, during which I was brought to recognize the artistic validity of my wife's point of view. I also learned from this encounter, and others that followed, that family Christmas rituals can carry the weight of law. Principles of tree decoration represent just one element in the emotional landscape of Christmas, the Ritual of All Rituals for most Americans. (In case you are wondering, my wife and I are now a tinsel-free family.)

December 25 was set as the day for Christmas by the Pope in the fourth century to correspond to the timing of the pagan winter solstice. By the Middle Ages, Christmas had become the major holiday of the year in Europe, but the festivities never lost their pagan roots. According to historians, Christmas became by an "annual indulgence in eating, dancing, singing, sporting, card playing, and gambling." Indeed, the Puritans who later came to North America were opposed to the festive aspects of Christmas and forbade the practice of the holiday.[1]

Most people don't know that Christmas did not become a major *family* holiday until the middle of the nineteenth century. Throughout most of western history, Christmas was more a community celebration than a family-centered tradition. True, people went to church and public festivities, and got together with their friends, but they did not engage in elaborate family meals and gift exchanges. When gifts *were* given, they tended to be special food items or small homemade artifacts. There were few Christmas trees in America until the mid-nineteenth century, and Santa was just starting to be a familiar character. The modern family Christmas with its elaborate family rituals and gift exchanges did not become popular until around 1880.[2]

The advent of Christmas as the quintessential family ritual celebration was a product of the early stirrings of the Psychological Family in the second half of the nineteenth century. As I described in Chapter 1, the Institutional Family of history had an outward community focus more than a inward family-centric one. Sunday, for example, was a communal day rather than a family day; so too was Christmas. The Psychological Family, which began to take root in the late nineteenth century and came to full flower in mid-twentieth century, was a more private group that emphasized its internal rituals and traditions. Family rituals require a degree of self-awareness as a distinct group with a history and a future, and most families did not have this kind of consciousness until the last 150 years. Before the modern era, according to historians, rituals and traditions were carried out in communities, not among individual families.[3]

Not only was Christmas not a family affair until recently, it was not primarily a religious ritual either. For its first 15 centuries, Christmas was dominated by secular fun and festivity rather than by religious practices related to the birth of Christ. Over the past century, Christmas became driven by the need for families to reunite and connect, and by marketers interested in selling their products to consumers. Religious elements have always been present, and to some people are the most important aspect of Christmas, but in general secular interests have held sway. Perhaps this helps explain why Christmas has become popular among non-Christians in so many parts of the world and is becoming the first truly global festival.[4]

But if family Christmas rituals got off to a late start historically, we have made up for lost time! Christmas has become the most structured private family ritual of them all, the internal equivalent of the highly scripted public family rituals of weddings and funerals. But the Christmas experience is a paradox: Although there are innumerable Christmas patterns and practices that are widely shared in American culture—such as to whom you must give gifts—there are innumerable variations that mark every family's Christmas—such as how to decorate the tree and when and how to open the presents. And because Christmas is about *memories and tradition* formed in childhood, even the smallest differences between two or more families' Christmas rituals can be jarring. In the midst of Christmas patterns formed in both the broader societal culture and one's own family culture, becoming intentional about Christmas offers a serious challenge. The first step is to understand the nature of the Christmas ritual dance that you already do.

I'LL BE HOME FOR CHRISTMAS

For families who celebrate Christmas, the location of the primary Christmas meal and gift exchange is even more consequential than for Thanksgiving because the emotional stakes are higher. Christmas traditions run deeper in the family psyche, and there is nothing like Christmas to bring family loyalties into clear and sometimes painful focus. Struggles may erupt months before the holidays when decisions are being made about where to celebrate.

Your in-laws are not your original family and their Christmas traditions are different from yours, so it's not unusual to feel left out and inclined to self-pity if you're at their house and everyone else seems to be having such a good time. The song does not say "I'll be at my in-laws for Christmas," leading to power struggles over whose house will host the main event, an issue discussed in the Thanksgiving chapter.

Societal norms state that the only "acceptable" reasons not to be with one's family at Christmas are that the geographical distance between you is too great or that you are with your spouse's family. Any other reason implies serious family problems. During 1984, the whole nation witnessed the president's family play this out. Ronald Reagan's son, Michael, was conspicuously absent from the family photograph at the president's California ranch. (Michael had no in-laws and presumably had the money to travel home.) Michael's stepmother, Nancy Reagan, said that her stepson was "estranged" from his father. Michael hotly and publicly denied this, insisting that the problem was really Nancy's excessive loyalty to her husband. Thus the nation was subjected to an all-American holiday squabble reflecting the mixed loyalties and wounded feelings that many American families experience at this time of year.

Even when there are no serious loyalty conflicts or family problems, practical impediments can make it difficult to spend Christmas with family. When Roger and Patricia were first married and lived far from both of their families, they alternated spending Christmas one year at her family's Nebraska farm, the next at his family's house in Philadelphia. Both families wanted them every year, of course. One year, in an excess of fair-minded zeal, they visited both families. They spent Christmas Eve in Philadelphia, then jetted cross-country on Christmas Day—including a few very "merry" hours at O'Hare Airport—in order to consume a second Christmas dinner in Nebraska. Roger was on crutches that year, and they had a new baby and a 2-year-old along.

As the children got older, Roger and Patricia began to realize that they needed and wanted to form their own family traditions at Christmas; they wanted to be more intentional about Christmas. The key trigger to this realization came when their 5-year-old daughter Emily asked, "How come Santa never comes to our house?" Her parents realized it was time to stay home for Christmas, a decision that their families reluctantly accepted. They did continue to visit their families right after Christmas some years, but they reserved Christmas Eve and Christmas Day for their nuclear family.

The Missing Link

Divorce can make where to spend Christmas location a tortuous decision. Even when divorced parents put their children's needs first, someone has to suffer losses and make sacrifices. When they focus instead on their own agendas, Christmas can become a crucible upon which to test children's loyalty. When parents remarry, the logistics are even more complex—a tangled muddle of new and old "family" members, households, and traditions—often comprising the makings of a holiday war. The bright side is that after a divorce or remarriage many families become more intentional about Christmas by developing new traditions. Children especially can be quite shrewd about the inherent possibilities in the new situation for extra attention and more food and presents.

Even when a family is lucky enough to escape loyalty struggles and divorce, it inevitably will deal with the death of parents and other family members. There is a special anguish about the first Christmas without a loved one, especially when it is the parent who hosted the Christmas celebrations. As with the loss of the Thanksgiving host, some families splinter at this point and never regenerate their familywide rituals at the holidays. The more fortunate accept new leadership from the next generation and maintain their family rituals.

When the loss is that of a younger parent or a child, Christmas is even more painful. Home may feel empty, not a site of celebration. The year after his wife Cindy died, my friend Peter Skipper and his three young children packed up and visited a close friend in California for Christmas holidays. In being intentional about their family Christmas, Peter, Cassie, Lonnie, and Petey were placing themselves in a different ritual space where they could celebrate Christmas as a new family creating new traditions. They knew Cindy would approve.

UNITED WE STAND, UNITED WE GET IRRITATED

The prevalent Christmas expectation is that we should be "merry," which is a state of mind that cannot be commanded or forced. In fact, the sheer intensity and duration of family Christmas rituals ensure long periods of anything but merriment. During the rest of the year, families respect regular patterns of contact, closeness, and distance, but at Christmastime, these interpersonal boundaries are overrun by swarming relatives and friends. Members of the extended family, who maintain a comfortable distance from each other by perhaps hundreds of miles throughout the year, now switch from phone calls and letters, individually initiated, to eyeball-to-eyeball contact, en masse. Peaceful neutrality, carefully nurtured through mutual avoidance of certain topics, breaks down under too much exposure. Previously tolerable differences among family members now become unbearable: The contemplative is bombarded by the incessant talker. The family socialist insists upon clarifying welfare issues to the Republican fund-raiser. The uncle cannot resist badgering his nephew about the new earring, and wondering what kind of parents would allow this "gender-bending." Merry Christmas, everyone.

As on Thanksgiving, on Christmas most families are expected to eat and drink themselves into a stupor, thus accounting for the torpidity of after-dinner conversation and the lethargy of Christmas afternoon, which runs neck and neck with Thanksgiving for the slowest afternoon of the year. Refer to my recommendations in the previous chapter for being intentional about planning to keep people in motion.

At Christmas, family members often find themselves clicking into old, familiar roles as if they'd never left home. One sister, the "princess" who never did any housework, manages once again to get out of doing the post-Christmas dinner dishes. She leaves them to the family "Cinderella," who quickly becomes passively resentful, as she used to. And most of the men go about their day as if showing up were their singular required contribution to the ritual.

And finally, there is the unspoken Christmas rule that conflict may simmer under the surface, but it must never erupt, because the one who starts the conflict will be accused of *ruining Christmas*. No one wants to be accused of *ruining Christmas*, a breach of conduct nearly on a par with ruining someone's wedding day. If Cinderella gets upset with Princess or with her lazy brother, somebody will quickly tell her that her negativity is out of line with the spirit of the holiday. If the conflict goes further, the family Guardian of Christmas Peace will signal, either directly or with tears or threats to leave, that the combatants should shut up and stop *ruining Christmas*. Thus, everyone accepts an uneasy truce—until next year when the old issues will no doubt rise once again to the surface.

'TIS BETTER TO GIVE—AND RECEIVE

Gifts are central to most Christmas traditions—and to the U.S. economy. American families spend an estimated 3 to 4 percent of their annual income on Christmas presents,[5] rather than make them, thus raising the stakes for businesses whose main profit comes at Christmas. The gift ritual—strategizing, shopping, purchasing, wrapping, and presenting—is without doubt the most nerve-wracking and exhausting aspect of the holidays for people. It's the gifts that make Christmas the family ritual without peer, the main event of the family year for those who celebrate it.

The exchanging of Christmas gifts was almost entirely ignored by social scientists until Theodore Caplow and his colleagues studied the ritual in their famous Middletown study in the late

1970s. They discovered through intensive interviews that very clear rules govern gift exchanges, rules that everyone seemed to understand but that no one could articulate. Ponder the following gift exchange rules that Caplow inferred from his interviews, and ask yourself if you already knew them implicitly, like rules of grammar.[6]

1. The Wrapping Rule: Christmas gifts must be wrapped before they are presented.

2. The Decoration Rule: Any room where Christmas gifts are distributed should be decorated by affixing seasonal paraphernalia to the wall, the ceiling, or the furniture.

3. The Gathering Rule: Christmas gifts should be distributed at gatherings where every person gives and receives gifts.

4. The Dinner Rule: Family gatherings at which gifts are distributed include a "traditional Christmas dinner."

5. The Gift Selection Rules: A Christmas gift should demonstrate the giver's familiarity with the receiver's preferences; surprise the receiver; and be scaled in economic value to the emotional value of the relationship. (An example of the latter would be that it would be unseemly to give one's nephew a gift of far greater value than the gift to one's son.)

6. The Scaling Rules: (These complex rules are stated in technical terms in Caplow's article. I paraphrase them here.)

   Husband-wife gifts are regarded as highest in value, followed by gifts from parents to children.

   Parents with more than one child should give them gifts of approximately equal value.

   Children do not give more expensive presents to parents than parents give to children.

   Treat your parents and parents-in-law equally.

Treat your married relatives' spouses equal to your relatives; for example, give your brother-in-law a gift roughly equal to the one you give your sister.

Gifts for siblings who live nearby and are part of one's network should be equal, but siblings with whom you share a less-close relationship may be given lesser gifts.

More distant relatives such as cousins, uncles, and aunts may be treated on a par with siblings if they are part of one's network.

Gifts to friends should not be valued more than gifts to spouses, parents, or children.

7. Fitness Rules: Rules about the appropriateness of gifts (women should not give cut flowers to men) are too numerous to specify, but one deserves attention here. Money is considered an appropriate gift from senior to junior kin (say, from grandparents to grandchildren) but not from junior to senior kin, regardless of the relative affluence of the parties.

8. The Reciprocity Rule: Participants should give at least one Christmas gift every year to their mothers, fathers, sons, daughters, to the current spouse of these persons, and to their own spouses. Participants expect to receive at least one gift in return from each of these persons, excepting infants. The Reciprocity Rule does not require the gifts to be of equal value. (Imbalance between the generations is central to the entire ritual, as parents give more than they receive from their young children.)

These Christmas rules for gift-giving are not written down anywhere; they are not found in etiquette books. And despite some variation among families of different ethnic groups, they appear to be widely followed in American society. They require so much complex balancing, however, that mistakes are also common, leading to regrets, misunderstandings, and bad feelings.

It's the Thought That Counts

Within these rules, there is still considerable room for individual styles of gift-giving, and for family variations. Every family, for example, puts its own spin on the fitness rules. Some families believe that extravagant, impulsive gifts best demonstrate their love: Your present is a diamond ring, a personal computer, or champion show dog—whether you wanted it or not. If both spouses share this proclivity, all is well, as long as they both understand the provisions of bankruptcy law. But if he comes from a "Christmas-extravagant" family, and she from a "Christmas-frugal" family, mutual consternation is inevitable. If, for example, the husband gives his wife a microwave oven with all the bells and whistles (when she's content with her 40-year-old gas stove), and she has bought him two ties and a beer mug, complications can result. He is hurt by her pointed lack of enthusiasm, while she feels overwhelmed by his gift, embarrassed by her own paltry offering, and resentful that he has somehow placed her in this untenable position.

Gift-giving is always a perilous undertaking, even when you try to follow the rules. Moving into a higher income bracket than the rest of the family, for example, sets in motion a real predicament. Presents of middling expense will be thought cheap: "With all that money he's raking in, you'd think my brother the doctor could get his only sister something a little nicer." On the other hand, expensive gifts will be branded crass and pretentious: "It was humiliating. She gave me a bottle of Chateau Lafite-Rothschild 1966, and I gave her a jug of Gallo Red undated."

And if the family network extends, the rules become vaguer, and it can be tricky to determine whether you are expected to keep giving gifts to certain people each year. If you have always exchanged gifts with your cousins, what about gifts to their children? To their children's new spouses? How far do you go? There are always possibilities for social gaffes, as when your second cousin, once removed, presents you with a leather-bound first edition, and you present him with . . . nothing. Next year, when you remedy the situation by getting him an antique silver snuffbox, he's already crossed you off his list.

Gifts carry messages to family members about what we think and expect of them, although some families simplify this by generically lumping certain members together—all men get socks or handkerchiefs, all women get kitchen appliances or bath oil. In other families, you are expected to engage in an intense personality study to find clues for the "perfect gift." Gifts can also communicate hostility or fear of change, as when a successful dieter receives two pounds of chocolates. Johnny Carson once told his television audience that he had never received so much alcohol for Christmas as he did the year he announced he was quitting drinking.

Another Opening, Another Show

When should Christmas gifts be opened? Christmas Eve, or Christmas morning? And, once the time is set, *how* should they be opened? According to elaborate structures or in donnybrooks of flying ribbon and paper? Growing up in Patricia's family, the gift-opening ceremony was on the elaborate side. The youngest child approached the tree first, picked up a present and handed it to the person whose name was on it. The whole family watched the opening of each gift, after which the receiver displayed the gift, commented on it, and expressed thanks. That person then selected and handed out the next present, in a stately choreography that could take hours. Roger felt like fainting with boredom.

Roger's family was at the opposite end of the ceremonial spectrum—verging on anarchy. Their procedure, which Roger was fond of, required about 90 seconds during which everyone ripped open their presents, expressed quick thanks, and scattered the contents all over the living room. Roger thought this ritual had two major advantages: You got to your presents quickly, and you didn't have to make a false show of delight over items you were lukewarm about. The first year Patricia sat through this orgy, she was shocked and nearly in tears. "I married into a pack of savages," she said to herself and later to Roger, who was not amused by the metaphor and so took the opportunity to comment on the annoying rigidity of her family's gift ritual.

In an unscientific survey of friends and acquaintances, I have discovered that the world is divided evenly into gift ceremonialists and gift anarchists. Unfortunately, the two groups tend to intermarry, as with the tinsel tossers, and they never, ever, talk about it before their first Christmas together.

THE CHRISTMAS COORDINATOR

Like any complex enterprise, Christmas requires a competent executive director, whom I call the Family Christmas Coordinator, the one person in most families who is in charge of putting the entire production together. Again, traditionally, this role belongs to the wife/mother of the family, so it is no accident that women's magazines begin in August to provide encyclopedic instructions for making, baking, and buying the perfect Christmas experience. For many women, Christmas is like a major athletic event, and August is not too soon to begin working out and making advance game plans.

Since family roles generally come in pairs, the Christmas Coordinator in this holiday dance is paired with the "Christmas Abstainer," usually a man (in heterosexual couples), who stays aloof from the demands of the season while being vaguely aware that the Coordinator is getting hard to live with. A predictable series of interactions between the Coordinator and the Abstainer begin soon after Thanksgiving. As the Coordinator becomes more obsessed with holiday preparations, the Abstainer becomes more detached and irritable, while the children for their part are becoming more excited and demanding.

Part of the Christmas Coordinator's burden is the belief that Christmas must come off perfectly, without a hitch, and approach a Yuletide fantasy of beautifully wrapped presents, Christmas carols sung on a frosty doorstep, freshly baked cookies, the fragrance of evergreens, the laughter of children, and so forth. There must be no undertone of irritation, no yelling, no drunks, no ungrateful relatives, no duplicate presents. This is a dream doomed to disappointment.

By Christmas Eve, the melodrama is underway, and usually is not being played according to the Coordinator's script. She is exhausted, worried about the outcome, annoyed by fault-finding relatives, and still hoping that the "pageant" will come off as promised. For months, she has shouldered the entire burden of Christmas, an unsung martyr who is growing tired of her cross. At last, appealing for help to the Abstainer, she breaks down in frustration, only to hear him accuse her of overreacting, getting worked up over nothing, flying off the handle.

The last section of this chapter offers suggestions for both the Coordinator and the Abstainer to prevent this common degeneration of the Christmas ritual.

SAME TIME NEXT YEAR

After Christmas, families wearily return to their normal patterns, and the Christmas Coordinator collapses, promising herself, never again. Like people two hours after a junk-food binge, many families experience a letdown after Christmas. They are relieved that the holiday is behind them, but they miss the intensity. Several months into the new year, a disease called "Christmas amnesia" sets in. In March or April, the Christmas Coordinator and her relatives forget about the ordeals, and begin to think fondly of next year's festivities; they even start jockeying for the right to celebrate Christmas in their own houses. This phenomenon is akin to women forgetting the pain of childbirth soon after delivery. It is an amnesia that helps to populate the earth and keep the tradition of family Christmas alive.

HAVE YOURSELF AN INTENTIONAL LITTLE CHRISTMAS

If your family celebrates Christmas, chances are you will do it again next year no matter how this year turned out. Except in extraordinary circumstances, the consequences of a complete boycott of family Christmas are just too grave. Nevertheless, there are options. If nothing else, you can work intentionally on your attitudes and expectations, which are three-fourths of what is good and bad about Christmas anyway. The following are my recommendations for accepting the inevitable hassles of Christmas while working toward enjoying it as an intentional family. Incorporate those that might work for your family and discard the others forthwith if they won't.

Expect the Traditional Difficulties

Families are very predictable. After observing Christmas festivities for a few years, you can pretty well predict that certain patterns will repeat. Your brother and sister-in-law will whine about having to miss their Mexico vacation to be with the family. Your sister and brother-in-law will let their children loose in your house. Your mother and father will snap at each other constantly, reflecting the strain of the season and the stickiness of too much family togetherness. Your uncle will tell his sister that their parents always favored her.

Since these behaviors are predictable, even scripted, in most families, why not expect them to show themselves—just as in Minnesota we expect the snow to fall every fall? If you anticipate these deviations from a "merry" Christmas, you will not let them ruin it. If it is a family Christmas, why not expect your family to act like, well, your family?

Plan for the Bad Moments

Some unpleasant events at Christmas can be tolerated only with Zenlike acceptance, but for others it is possible to formulate in advance a plan of action. As on Thanksgiving, you can't prevent a post-Christmas dinner slump, but you can take the edge off it by proposing a family outing. And before the meal, have a variety of board games in reserve, to pull out when your sister starts her traditional monologue about how hard she works in her job, or when Aunt Margaret and Uncle George begin their annual debate about whether the Catholic Church should have ever abandoned the Latin Mass. Scrabble, anyone? The point is, take advantage of family predictability by generating schemes to ward off the ill winds or at least to minimize the damage.

Leopards May Change Their Spots

Don't be so locked into your expectations of family members that you fail to notice, and celebrate, when they act "out of character." After surviving a heart attack in the fall, Grandpa may be downright sentimental this Christmas, unlike his Scroogelike demeanor of past years. Be open to the change. He may be willing to talk about his childhood Christmases, giving you an unprecedented glimpse into past family traditions. The balancing act for families at Christmas is to prepare for the norm, while being open to the unpredictable.

Get the Christmas Coordinator a Supporting Cast

Coordinating Christmas can be a rewarding experience, as long as one person doesn't carry the whole burden. For many Christmas Coordinators, it's not just the workload that gets them down, it's the awesome responsibility of decision-making. Buying presents for your in-laws might be a chore, but one that becomes a burden when your spouse won't even make suggestions about what to give them. Tell him (I am assuming that the Coordinator is female, and the Abstainer male) that he has to share in the decision-making—and the shopping as well—for gifts for his family and for your common children.

The Christmas Coordinator can politely inform family members in advance that you want help this year on meal preparation, setup, and cleanup. And then write down specific names for specific tasks. It is best to solicit these commitments in advance, so you don't come across as a Christmas Shrew by losing your temper when people haven't volunteered. Avoid this: "Do I have to do everything around here? Why don't you get off your lazy butts and help for a change?" People will shape up—temporarily—but wonder what happened to your Christmas spirit. If the Coordinator involves others in the planning and work, everyone has a better time. Maximum participation is a cornerstone of successful family rituals.

Slowly Involve the Christmas Abstainer

I say "slowly" because the Christmas Coordinator is often ambivalent about giving up control over events. The Abstainer should not announce: "I'm tired of your complaints, so this year, I will buy the kids' presents"; or, "This year, I've decided to cook the turkey and fix the trimmings." The first statement will be viewed by the Christmas Coordinator as a unilateral takeover of a valued role, and the second as criticism of her past performance in preparing the Christmas meal. Both are doomed to cause conflict, which then justifies to the Abstainer his right to slack off.

It is much better for the Abstainer to begin by proving himself a reliable helper for the Christmas chores: writing Christmas cards; thinking about, shopping for, and wrapping presents; preparing part of the meal, and cleaning up after it. Breaking out of the Abstainer role is best done gradually, perhaps by helping with one or two tasks the first year, and then adding others the next year. Eventually, he may start to enjoy the season more through being active. And his spouse will learn to trust his commitment enough to really share the responsibility. But keep in mind that real partnership in decision-making comes only after the Abstainer has shown that he can actively support and appreciate the Coordinator's efforts.

Honor Traditions, But Experiment with Change

Tradition and continuity are what give Christmas its special quality. Changes thus are best introduced with delicacy and respect for other family members' emotional attachments to the traditional ways. New daughters-in-law and sons-in-law bring different family traditions into the family but they are wise to step carefully before suggesting that their way be incorporated. Even after a new family member has convinced his or her spouse of the value of the alternative ritual, it is prudent to avoid taking too much personal leadership for instigating the change. Rather, the "blood" family member might suggest a "small" change—as "an experiment for this year." For example, if you want to slow down the gift exchange, perhaps suggest that this year the children open their presents one by one, for all to see. Then let the adults have their orgy of tearing off wrapping paper. The ritual will have been slowed down, and the adults will have the opportunity to assess the new way, without having to make a complete shift the first time.

Discuss Gift Exchange Expectations in Advance

Intentional families are able to work out agreements on managing gift exchanges for the larger family clan. True, some families continue to give everyone presents, but this is too expensive and time-consuming for most families, who must negotiate Christmas ground rules for the process.

The White family, for example, puts the adults' names into a hat. Each adult member draws a name and is expected to purchase a gift of no more than $50 for that individual. Unless the family becomes intentional about its gift ritual, for most families, the expense and time involved in planning, shopping, purchasing, and wrapping Christmas presents soon undermines the joy of the season. Even for couples, it can be helpful to give each other a clue about the magnitude of Christmas gifts you are considering. Leah and I have this kind of discussion each year, which prevents either of us from feeling bad about not having reciprocated the other's generosity in quantity or value of gifts.

Create New Christmas Rituals in Single-Parent Families or Stepfamilies

A new family structure can be reinforced by creating new ways to celebrate Christmas, ways that were not present in the previous family structure. For post-divorce families, the children and both parents can decide, for example, that Christmas Eve will be with Mom and her family, and Christmas Day with Dad and his family. Perhaps they can plan different activities on those days than they did during the time that Mom and Dad were married. This might mean starting to sing Christmas carols, or going to a different church, or going to brunch on Christmas Day.

Similarly, for stepfamilies, it is important that aspects of both parents' traditions be reflected in Christmas, plus some brand-new rituals that neither family shared in the past. The challenge is to cling to the old ways, while introducing the new to create a sense of being a special family with your own traditions.

Don't Be Alone

Most of what I have written assumes that you are in regular contact with your family. Sadly, though, there are families totally out of touch, often because of major trauma such as abuse or neglect, splits over marrying outside one's religious or racial group, or coming out as gay or lesbian. Being cut off from one's parents or children is among the most painful experience of all. When such an estrangement has occurred, I do not recommend the risk of trying to mend fences on Christmas Eve. But it can be helpful to find at least one relative to connect with at Christmas, in addition to the friends who have become your new intentional family. People too readily assume their whole family is involved in the estrangement. You might reach out to one of your siblings who has not taken sides in the family feud, or to a cousin, an aunt, or an uncle. This connection might be no more than a phone call on Christmas Day, or a short visit. But any family contact at Christmas is generally far better than none whatsoever. The best way to ease the pain of a family alienation at Christmas is to engage with at least one relative who can give you a sense of linkage to your past—and some hope that the future may be different.

If a family Christmas requires so much physical and psychological labor, and carries the risk of so many things going wrong, why do it? Why not just forget the whole season, hole up with work or hobbies, exchange no presents, and leave town? The reason is that Christmas, if it is part of your family tradition, is the one time in the year when you are expected to connect—even if only through a card or phone call—with everyone else in your family system. Christmas calls our families together once a year, and when we reconnect, we are pulled along, for a few days at least, by the same currents and we breathe the same air. We celebrate new and growing members of the clan, and we observe and mourn the decline and loss of other members. We take stock of where we have traveled. Although Christmas has become commercialized and trivialized in contemporary America, many of us would feel impoverished without it. We need a festival that combines the powerful elements of religion, culture, family, and the winter solstice. We need a protracted family ritual that society makes possible by creating time off from work and school. We need a time to pursue ideals of family harmony and solidarity, even if the reality inevitably falls short. As Garrison Keillor wrote, "A lovely thing about Christmas is that it's compulsory, like a thunderstorm, and we all go through it together. . . ."[7] Despite its faults, if we did not have Christmas, we would have to invent it.

Community and Religious Rituals

My wife's important family rituals were also community rituals. On the night of someone's birthday, family friends and relatives all showed up for the party. No one was formally invited or even informed about the celebration; they just "showed up" for birthdays, wedding anniversaries, and graduations.

When my wife first told me about these rituals of community, I could hardly believe her. I understood how relatives might come without invitations to a birthday party or an anniversary celebration, but neighbors and friends as well? That meant everyone in the network was keeping track of one another's special days, and making sure their time was free on the date. And they assumed that the family would expect them to arrive without a prior conversation or invitation.

The host family, for its part, would prepare food for the anticipated large gathering. It included more than birthday cake and ice cream; there were Danish open-faced sandwiches, cookies, other sweets, milk for the children, and coffee. When I asked Leah how her family managed not to have too little or too much food, she said it was never a problem. People in her community knew one another's schedules; if someone was out of town and couldn't come, Leah's parents would know it. Otherwise, they could count on everyone's presence and support at a family event.

Counting on one another's presence and support—this is the heart of community. Families badly need this kind of community of extended family, friends, religious fellowships, neighborhoods, school groups, and other social organizations. The now overused phrase "It takes a village to raise a child" conveys the central importance of community for nurturing family life.

Traditionally, writing about family rituals has focused on those within the family. But in recent years, many observers of both the family and broader American society have concluded that weakening of community ties lies at the heart of family and other social ills. The kind of community my wife experienced as a child would be regarded with astonishment in our fragmented, urbanized society.

BOWLING ALONE

The political scientist Robert Putnam has popularized a metaphor for this decline in community in the United States since the 1960s: "bowling alone." He notes that whereas more people bowl in the United States in the 1990s than in the 1960s, there has been a drastic decline in bowling league participation. We now bowl alone, or with a single friend. Significantly bowling leagues involve a commitment to other people to show up on a particular night every week to support the team. They are an organized form of community involvement.[1]

When I was a novice family therapist, I remember a father declining a Tuesday evening slot—normally, a premium after-work appointment on the only evening I worked—because his bowling league met that night. Although he was ready to take time off work some other day, I wondered whether his reluctance to schedule our sessions on his bowling night was an indication of the priority his family had in his mind. He replied that the team had lost its only substitute player, and that if he dropped out, they would forfeit all their matches. I was unimpressed.

But looking back on that conversation, I am unimpressed with my response. Like many therapists, my focus was on the small world of the family and not on broader community ties, and especially not on community obligations such as following through on a promise to a team to be there every week and do one's best.

Only in more recent years have more therapists discovered the importance of community connections for the well-being of families and their members. In the past we treated families as if they live in a fishbowl and not in an ocean; we have since learned that family health and community health are thoroughly interwoven.[2]

But if family solidarity is tied to community solidarity, then we are in serious trouble. Putnam, along with other observers, has documented a major decline in civic participation and social involvement in American communities over the past generation. Putnam's summary:

> Surveys of average Americans in 1965, 1975, and 1985, in which they recorded every single activity during a day—so-called time-budget studies—indicate that since 1965, time spent on informal socializing and visiting is down (perhaps by one-quarter), and time devoted to clubs and organizations is down even more sharply (by roughly half). Membership records of such diverse organizations as the PTA, the Elks club, and the League of Women Voters, the Red Cross, labor unions, and even bowling leagues show that participation in many conventional voluntary associations has declined by roughly 25 percent to 50 percent over the last two to three decades. Surveys show sharp declines in many measures of collective political participation, including attending a rally or speech (off 36 percent between 1973 and 1993), attending a meeting on town or school affairs (off 39 percent), or working for a political party (off 56 percent).[3]

The traditional Institutional Family was based firmly in community, with most people spending their entire lives in one farming area, where people lived more in the public arena than in their cramped family quarters. Think of the movie *Fiddler on the Roof*, which depicts the intricate interweaving of family and village in nineteenth-century Russia. The Psychological Family of the twentieth century turned the family inward at the same time it raised the ante for what we expect of family life. Community involvement became voluntary. But the generation of the mid-twentieth century was involved in substantial ways in community and civic life, according to Putnam. Participation may have been more voluntary than in the Institutional Family, but many families signed up nonetheless for civic engagement in groups such as the PTA, the Elks, the VFW, political parties, labor unions, the Red Cross, and church organizations.[4]

The precipitous decline in community involvement began during the late 1960s, the same period that the Psychological Family was giving way to the Pluralistic Family. American individualism, in the past balanced by a strong commitment to community involvement, began to dominate the culture as never before. And families became increasingly more isolated from their networks of support. In a handful of generations, we moved from highly interdependent farming communities to urban neighborhood communities, where people knew the names of every adult and child on their block, to suburban enclaves without sidewalks where it is rare that people know the names of neighbors three houses down the block.[5]

The Ties That Bind

Intentional Families find ways to counteract the isolation of contemporary American life, especially those from ethnic groups who have a stronger history of extended family and community ties. African-American families, for example, have generally emphasized the support of extended family such as grandparents and aunts and uncles. And along with traditional American Indian families, African-American families also have a strong tradition of "fictive kin," people who, although not related by blood, marriage, or adoption, are nevertheless regarded as family members. Likewise, many Hispanic and Asian-American families have strong links to extended fam-

> The good news is that we are more free to create our communities. The bad news is that most of us are unsure how in a society that splinters more than unites.

ily and their community. And many families of gays and lesbians—families who are suspect to many in the larger society—are well-connected within their own communities. Intentional Families are often formed through bonds other than marriage or blood.

Mainstream American culture, however, pulls us toward more individualism, more separation from community, resulting in more family instability. (This trend is even stronger in poor neighborhoods, which commonly lack strong neighborhood and other social structures.) These downsides, however, present the opportunity to create intentional communities. The good news is that we are more free to create our communities. The bad news is that most of us are unsure how in a society that splinters more than unites.

FROM SOCIAL ACTIVITIES TO COMMUNITY RITUALS

In the late 1970s, when our children were small, Leah and I began to get together with three other families from our church whose children were of similar ages. At first, we were just social friends who enjoyed one another's company; they were part of our social network, but we did not yet share any rituals of community.

I don't remember how it started, but after about a year, a ritual evolved that brought us together as a group eight times per year, in addition to those times we saw one another at church and on a one-to-one basis. We decided to celebrate each of the adults' birthdays during the year, half the time with our children, and half the time without. We rotated among one another's homes for these celebrations. We gave joke gifts, we embellished a group apron that we passed on to the birthday person, and we decorated that person's lawn with ugly ornaments, including pink flamingoes and plastic chipmunks.

After a couple of years, we decided we needed a name for our group. The inspiration came from Leah, who would sometimes accept compliments in a way uncharacteristic for midwesterners with the expression "Damn, I'm good!" The line became a standard, and our group name was derived from it: "Diggers," a condensation of "'Damn I'm Good'ers."

What made the Diggers' time together an experience of community was our ritual birthday celebrations, which involved the three elements of ritual: repetition, coordination, and significance. They gave us the chance to develop bonds, and gave us a sense of identity as a group of families. Finally, the ritual required a commitment that no one shirked over a period of several years, until two families moved away and the Diggers dissolved.

Making a commitment to community rituals is difficult for families in a society that encourages people to do their own thing. A community ritual, like family rituals, requires a willingness to be present and active no matter how you are feeling that day. My friend Patrick dislikes being on public display, but he organizes a block party in his neighborhood every year because he believes this ritual generates community spirit and because he wants his children to know

> Making a commitment to community rituals is difficult for families in a society that encourages people to do their own thing.

that community relationships are formed through effort and leadership. It's the difference between calling up friends and inviting them over at a time that is convenient for both of you, versus making a pledge to get together at regularly scheduled times. My friend Elizabeth belongs to a church group made up of couples who support one another's marriages and encourage community by celebrating everyone's wedding anniversaries during the year. This kind of commitment marks the difference between an optional social activity and a community ritual.

COMMUNITY SERVICE RITUALS

The Roberts family is proud of their neighborhood for sponsoring a block party every year. It happens because the Roberts and several other families take responsibility for it. They plan the date at least six months in advance, they get the permit, organize the activities, and involve the rest of the neighbors. While those in this planning group have forged friendships over the years, the block party is not a ritual of friendship in the narrow sense. It is a ritual of community that involves everyone in the three-block neighborhood; it is the one time in the year when all doors are open and no one needs an excuse to talk to a neighbor. The people who participate, and particularly the people who plan it, feel a connection beyond living near one another.

Many Americans do volunteer work that contributes to their communities, but they tend to be involved as individuals rather than as families. Causing a typical conflict, weekend volunteer work at a homeless shelter, for example, takes parents away from their own home and children. The solution is to combine family and community rituals by volunteering as a family.

> The Walsh family volunteers as a group on a regular basis at a child-care center for homeless families. The Walsh children, a boy 14 and a girl 12, are old enough to contribute fully. This gives them a way to enact their family values in their community, while at the same time building their connections as a family. (If I were coaching them, I would urge them to be even more intentional about their family ritual of community by going out for a soft drink afterward to process the experience.) The Walshes have also become close to the staff at the shelter, thus expanding their community even further.

> Judy Hostader, a single parent of a preschool child, volunteers at her daughter's Head Start program in the afternoon on her days off, where she spends time working with her daughter's group. Her weekly ritual gives the staff time to plan enrichment activities for the children, it exposes the children to someone new to work with, it demonstrates to Judy's daughter that she must "share" her mother, and it expands Judy's community to include the program staff and other parents.

Sue and Steve Anthony mentor young couples in the premarriage workshops at their church, and they are lay leaders of marriage enrichment workshops. Now with teenage children, their own marital journey has not been easy. Steve was actively alcoholic for 15 years before getting help, during which time he had affairs. Sue learned to take full responsibility for the children and to cover up for their father. But this couple and family rallied, got help, recovered, and became a highly Intentional Family. Sue and Steve bring both their experience and their insight to their mentoring role. Helping other couples, of course, strengthens further their own connection, and gives them the sense that their difficulties have been turned to good purpose.

No Time Like the Present

When I ask people at family ritual workshops about their community rituals, they frequently mention the problem of lack of time. Time constraints no doubt are a major challenge for all families, but perhaps the main problem is how they are spending their leisure time. Most Americans spend many hours a day watching television instead of being involved in their communities or talking with their family members. Indeed, Robert Putnam has marshaled evidence that television watching may be the single most important source of the decline in civic engagement since the 1960s. In 1995, the hours spent watching television were 50 percent higher than in the

> If TV diminishes family rituals in both home and community, then becoming intentional about its use may be the first order of business for Intentional Families.

1950s, and each successive generation watches more than the previous one. The more hours a person spends watching television, the less he or she is socially involved. It isn't just the time commitment, however, because more newspaper reading is associated with increased civic engagement. Unlike other hobbies, television reduces social involvements. Putnam summarizes: "TV watching comes at the expense of nearly every social activity outside the home, especially social gatherings and informal conversations. TV viewers are homebodies."[6]

Earlier, I made the case that TV watching also reduces ritualized family interactions in the home. If TV diminishes family rituals in both home and community, then becoming intentional about its use may be the first order of business for Intentional Families.

FAMILIES AND RELIGIOUS RITUALS OF COMMUNITY

For American families across all income strata and ethnic groups, religion provides a primary source of rituals of community. The great majority of American families belong to a religious organization of some sort, and on a typical weekend 41 percent of all families with children attend a religious service.[7] In addition, families who are members of religious institutions also are more active in nonreligious community groups and organizations than are people who do not affiliate with a religious institution. In other words, religiously active families tend to be involved in all sorts of rituals of community.[8]

Going to a weekend religious service is a major family ritual in American life. At its best, it connects a family with a special community of belief and support. At its worst, it is a battleground between parents and children over whether the children "have to go."

When Leah and I were new parents living far away from our families, our church community gave us an important source of support, different from that of friends our own age, most of whom did not have children. The church gathered families at all stages in life, including experienced parents who took an interest in us and our babies. What I remember best were the conversations at coffee hour when Leah and I would talk about pregnancy and babies with people who knew what we were talking about.

Joan, a fellow church member, was our prepared childbirth teacher. As she greeted us every Sunday after the service, with her own school-aged children running about, I remember feeling hopeful about parenthood because of the joy she exuded in being a mother. She had six children and sometimes looked harried, but never without a sense of joy. Of course, I asked her how she had the time for six children. I will never forget her reply, which summarized her sense of commitment as a parent: "One child takes all your time, so six can't take any more." Judy proved to be a firm guide and teacher. I remember her gently reprimanding me after I made a comment (I think it was about another woman's delivery complications) that she thought was inappropriate for Leah to hear just before her due date. I nodded and immediately stopped my story, an atypical show of compliance on my part that testified to my respect for Judy as a more experienced member of our religious community.

What were the odds of us having someone like Judy and the other families be part of our community if we were not involved in a religious organization? Not very great. We could have tried to create a three-generational community around ourselves, but this would have been a full-time job for a struggling young couple who were new to the area. A neighborhood community would also have

> The most widely available source of family rituals of community is a church, synagogue, or mosque.

been a possibility, but generally there are not weekly rituals of connection in most neighborhoods during which you can interact with dozens of people at different phases of the life cycle. The reality is that the most widely available source of family rituals of community is a church, synagogue, or mosque.

It takes more than just showing up, however, to develop a religious community. Attending services can be a valuable experience through the public enactment of the family's faith. However, if the family does not participate in the rest of the congregation's life, the experience of community will be limited. Although we enjoyed and benefited from the church services when our children were small, it was coffee hour that I remember most. And coffee hour in turn was meaningful because we were involved in other activities and committees in the church. We knew these families because we worked together to maintain and build our religious community. The coffee hour became our weekly ritual of connection, and a cornerstone of my family's community life when our children were babies.

Overcoming Barriers

Religious community life is not without its shortcomings. Some congregations are so couple-oriented, for example, that single people, and especially divorced people, do not feel welcome or comfortable. The same is true for homosexual people in many mainstream religious denominations. For families of mixed faiths, too, religion can be a source of division as well as a missed opportunity for common rituals of community. And some individuals have had such negative childhood experiences with religious institutions that they are not open to religious experiences as adults.

I encourage people with negative religious experiences to become intentional about seeking out a community that better meets their needs and beliefs. There is tremendous diversity among American religious communities today, enabling almost anyone willing to become involved to find a spiritual home. For the newly divorced, there are congregations offering support groups. There are congregations that welcome lesbian parents and their child. For those turned off by the rigidity of religion, there are highly flexible congregations available—often within the same denomination or faith tradition. True, the religious community that fits you or your family may not necessarily be the one across the street. You may have to investigate, talk to friends, and travel around to find it. But if you are intentional about creating family rituals of religious community, you will find a community that fits your needs and that can use your support. If you are not religious or cannot find a religious community for your family, then your challenge is to find alternative communities that share your values.

Do I Have to Go?

Family religious rituals of community face the inevitable conflicts with children who don't want to go to religious education classes and to weekly services. In an age of television entertainment and video games, religious institutions must compete for children's attention. This is especially true as children approach their teen years, when their boredom quotient peaks along with their need to sleep in on weekends. If your religious community does not have creative children's programs, then you are likely at some point to find your children resisting or refusing to go.

Weekly battles over attending religious services, like struggles over all family rituals, can undermine the power of this family religious ritual of community. On the other hand, simply giving in to a reluctant child can deprive the family of a way to collectively enact its values. Children should not be given the power to pull the plug on an important family ritual. But that's not to say that children's needs and preferences don't count. Following are recommendations for dealing with resistant children:

- Find out what your child does not like about the religious services or religious education program. There may be specific issues that can be remedied, or at least waited out, such as a teacher the child doesn't like.
- If you agree with your child that the services are not responsive enough to children's needs, or that the religious education program is lacking, then discuss your concerns with leaders in your religious organization. Volunteer to investigate how to improve children's programming. This is especially crucial for teenagers, who need adults with special abilities in relating to youth.

- If your child only vaguely claims that the service or classes are "dumb" or "boring," then try participating more actively in the child's education. Get a copy of the curriculum and discuss the content with your child, or describe to your child in advance what will be taking place in the service. This strategy works better with younger children than with teenagers.

- Pay attention to the messages you and your co-parent are giving regarding religious matters. If Mom goes to services regularly but Dad does not, then your child is getting a mixed message about the importance of religion as a family ritual. Boys in particular discover that religious participation is more a female thing, and they are backed by statistics: 28 percent of American men report attending a religious service on a typical weekend, as compared to 46 percent of women.[9] In divorced families, do the children only go with Mom on her weekend? There may be little the religious parent can do in such a situation, but I encourage frank discussion about what the parents value for their children and what the parents can do together to represent those values.

- Be clear what is mandatory and what is optional religious participation for your children. If you decide that your children will participate in family religious rituals of community, then tell them so and enforce your policy. Don't bargain every week.

- Consistent attendance is an important way to avoid arguments, whereas deciding every weekend whether or not to attend services invites a reluctant child to make a weekly case for staying home. Again, rituals involve predictability. Building religious community activities into your life on a routine basis gives them ritual power, if the element of significance is also present. Dabbling in a religious community will encourage your children to resist when they don't feel like attending.

- Decide at what age your children can decide for themselves whether to attend services or religious education. Some parents tell their children that in high school they can decide whether to join the family for religious activities; for other families, it is age 16 or 18, or when the child leaves home. Whatever you decide, be clear about your expectations, explain your rationale for them, but refuse to debate their merits over and over again.

- Don't let your child sabotage the family ritual by demonstrations of boredom or disinterest. You can't stop your teenager from looking like he or she would rather be sitting on a bed of hot coals than listening to a sermon, but you can take away the power of this look to interfere with your enjoyment of the service. If you have satisfied yourself that your religious community is doing what it can to be sensitive to your children's religious and personal needs, then don't let your child's attitude undermine the family ritual. Avoid reprimanding your child for having a "bad attitude," since you can't directly affect your child's attitude anyway. You can challenge your children's behavior—being late getting ready for services for example—but not their attitudes or feelings about religion or religious services. Commanding a child to change an attitude (as distinguished from a behavior) just invites the child to dig in further, or to fake a positive attitude.

When parents truly value their family rituals of religious community, the religious organization is making a good effort to reach out to children and youth, and the parents have made a clear, nondebatable policy about family participation, then children have the necessary foundation from which to gain something of value from their years of involvement in religious activities with their families.

Healing Rituals for Families and Religious Communities

Contemporary families are left to traverse their life course with too little community support for healing and commitment. Religious communities in particular have untapped resources for creating rituals that help families affirm their bonds and heal from losses and life transitions. Congregations could support marriages by celebrating wedding anniversaries of congregants through rituals that allow for public reaffirmation of commitment. They could support divorcing families through rituals of mourning, forgiving, letting go, and re-commitment to shared parenting. They could hold regular rituals of grieving for families who have had losses, rather than just relying on the traditional funeral ritual. They could help families ritualize their mixed emotions when a child leaves home or when an aging parent enters a nursing home.

These rituals can be conducted with groups of families who share similar experiences, and might best be created through the collaboration of clergy, members of the congregation, and mental health professionals such as family therapists. This combination of ritual creators can bring spiritual depth, psychological depth, and grounding in the real needs of families.

The next chapter continues the discussion of family rituals of community by examining in detail the two major public rituals of family life—weddings and funerals. In Chapter 11, Intentional Single Parents and Remarried Families, we discuss a major public ritual of family life for observant Jewish people—the bar mitzvah and bat mitzvah.

Rituals of Passage:
Weddings and Funerals

Most family rituals occur at home, away from the gaze and judgment of the community. No one is around to evaluate the quality of your family dinner or bedtime rituals. But weddings and funerals are planned by the family to share with their community, which is why they are so packed with meaning and stress.

Weddings and funerals have always been public events because they are too important to be left to individuals. We all have a stake in the start of a new family and in the death of a member of the community. But being intentional about these two central family rituals, in the face of community traditions and pressures, is a major challenge for families.

WEDDINGS

Wedding rituals occur in every human society because marriage in its various forms has enormous social significance. In the Western world, the weddings of royalty and the upper class were always highly ritualized because of their political importance. By the eighteenth century, families of the middle class were also celebrating weddings in a big way. But it wasn't until the nineteenth century in Europe and America that almost all families, rich and poor, began putting substantial time and resources into weddings. It was during this period that what we think of as the "traditional wedding" came into being.

The traditional wedding is American society's classic example of a rite of passage. Anthropologists studying premodern cultures realized that rituals served as transitions from one state of being to another, for example, from childhood to adolescence. (Confirmations and bar mitzvahs serve the same purpose today for Christians and Jews, respectively.) Traditional rites of passage involved a separation from the community, a transitional event, and then reemergence with a new social identity. In other words, you go away, you are transformed, and you return with a new role in the community.[1] Traditional wedding ceremonies involved all three stages.

Although there are regional, ethnic, and religious variations, the general outline of a traditional American wedding ceremony is as follows: At the outset, the groom stands at the front the church with his best man, awaiting his bride. Before that, he has been mingling about, whereas the bride is in seclusion getting prepared. Immediate family members are escorted to their assigned places on either side of the aisle. There is a pause. The rite of transition begins in earnest when the music shifts and the bride's party starts walking down the aisle. The first high point of the ritual occurs when the bride appears, resplendent in a white gown, accompanied by her father or other significant man. The couple are reunited at the front when the parents hand her over to her groom. The rite of transition culminates with the couple's exchange of vows in solemn tones in front of a member of the clergy. Sometimes at the end of the service, particularly if the woman has taken the man's family name, the clergyperson introduces the couple to the congregation as Mr. and Mrs. They are now legally and religiously married, with all the accompanying rights and responsibilities, before God and the state. The transformation of identity now complete, the couple walk back down the aisle in more informal fashion to joyous music. The receiving line then initiates the postceremony rituals of congratulations and celebration.

However, this traditional wedding ritual is packed with a number of fascinating contradictions:[2]

- *Traditional weddings are public ceremonies that are neverthe-less organized by individual families.* Virtually every other public ceremony in our society is organized by clergy, officials, or other professionals. No wonder families feel so much pressure, and why they rely on wedding guides and other "expert" opinions.

- *Weddings follow strict guidelines of propriety, with a personal touch.* Dear Abby and Ann Landers have made a living responding to irate family members and guests who all have complaints about violations of wedding protocol, everything from the invitations to what the bride wore and the lack of thank-you notes. Although there are clear rights and wrongs in traditional weddings, the couple is also expected to put its own stamp on the ritual in details such as the invitations, flowers, cake, music, wedding attire, vows, and order of service. These personal choices must also be "correct," that is, not out of line with community expectations. The double-bind is thus manifest: To be unoriginal is to not measure up, but to be too original is to invite social disapproval.

- *Even couples with little religious affiliation often want religious weddings.* Couples who do not make time for the "sacred" in their daily lives nevertheless frequently want this religious aspect to their weddings. In American society, only religious surroundings make possible the traditional wedding pomp and circumstance of the majestic bridal procession up a long aisle, high-vaulted ceilings, the engulfing organ music, and the sense that something profound and holy is occurring. An office wedding by a justice of the peace carries far less ritual power. The traditional wedding ritual is even more potent if held at the place of one's baptism, bar mitzvah or bat mitzvah, and the weddings and funerals of loved ones. The walls reverberate with family memories.

- *Traditional religious weddings combine the sense of the sacred and the sexual, elements that are rarely connected in society.* In all cultures and all religions, the sexual bond is what makes marriage unique. Sexual themes, therefore, pervade the wedding ritual, from the presumed virginity of the bride in her white gown and the readings from the erotic Song of Songs in the Bible to the expectation that the bride and groom will exchange a lover's kiss. The couple is expected to consummate their union on the wedding night. Traditional religious rituals also refer to the outcome of their sexual activity—children, the continuity of the family, and the community. Failure to consummate the marriage is in fact grounds for annulment in most religions. This combination of the sacred and the sexual gives weddings special power in our consciousness.

• *The couple are elevated and celebrated by the community, but also teased and embarrassed*. After honoring the bride and groom with gifts and special attention, guests at the traditional wedding reception expect the couple to submit to embarrassing, silly rituals such as feeding each other cake, dancing on command, having people pay to dance with them, removing and tossing a garter belt, having to kiss whenever the guests tinkle their glasses, and enduring practical jokes as they prepare to leave for their honeymoon. The same kinds of rituals occur in many other cultures; in Hindu weddings, for example, the couple is required to play various games for the benefit of the guests. It is as if the community wants to remind the couple not to feel above those who know and love them the best.

• *Weddings in contemporary society are expected to bring a man and woman together as equal partners in marriage, but the traditional ceremony suggests an imbalance*. The bride's white dress is the key symbol. The white color symbolizes youth and virginity, two elements not regarded as important for the groom. She purchases her dress, often at considerable expense, and is expected to keep it. The groom generally rents his tuxedo unless he happens to own one. The bride is the object of much more attention than the groom before, during, and after the ceremony. In the traditional ceremony, she is given away by her family; no one gives him away. In the past, she received a ring; he did not. In many cases, she still changes her family name to his. All of these elements make it clear that the change in identity is more significant for the woman than for the man, implying that her status in the world will be dependent on his. Although most contemporary couples aspire to equality in marriage, they enthusiastically go through a ritual that emphasizes the woman's inequality.[3]

• *Traditionally only first marriages are allowed the full ritual.* Actually, the key is the bride's prior marriages, not the groom's. A woman supposedly only has the right to wear white once. After that, she is expected to be more discreet about what she wears—she is clearly no longer a virgin—and what she expects in the way of attention and gifts. If the man has been married three times before but the woman has never been married, they are still eligible to have a traditional wedding—another clear illustration of how a wedding is thought to change a woman's identity more than a man's. But Intentional Couples today sometimes ignore these strictures for second marriages and have all the bells and whistles at their wedding. I know one woman who had eloped for her first wedding and decided to do make the second one a grand production. It was her groom's first marriage and he was all for it. (Chapter 11 contains other ideas about second marriages.)

WHOSE WEDDING IS IT ANYWAY?

In our individualistic age, it is possible to overlook an important truth about weddings, especially first weddings: Namely, that they are as much for the families and the community as for the couple. Historically, most marriages were arranged by the families, who chose the partners and dictated the celebration. Even today, for parents, seeing their children married "well" is seen as the last great test of their success in childrearing—even if the child is 37 and a corporate vice president. For the bride's mother, it may be her chance to plan a wedding, if she was not permitted to plan her own (her own mother having done the honors). For both families, it's a chance to assemble the clan for a joyful occasion. Beyond family, it's a chance to assemble friends who have been part of the couple's lives. A wedding is a time for the community to celebrate and for two families to build bridges through their young members.

That their wedding has many purposes may only occur to the engaged couple when they begin discussions about the guest list—how big it should be and who should be on it. That's also when they realize the truth in the adage that blood is thicker than anything else. Uncle Alvin, whom the bride can hardly remember meeting, must be sent an invitation and given a place of honor, whereas her old friend from eighth grade has to be cut. When the bride and groom suggest a folk song and guitar for the service, the bride's mother has a meltdown because of the reaction she anticipates from the religiously conservative wing of the family. Thus, the bride and groom have to decide how far to push for innovation and their own wishes in the face of their parents' convictions and concerns.

Weddings, too, are occasions for reflection by guests and participants alike about the marriages that have shaped their lives. I know this was the case when I gave the wedding sermon for friends, for whom I had been appointed legal minister for a day so that they could be married in their Unitarian-Universalist church during the summer when the minister was away. As a marital therapist, I had presided over a number of divorces, and I must say, the wedding was much more rewarding. Following is the text of my remarks, which were brief because of the 105-degree heat that June day in Iowa City.

> I want to speak today to everyone except the bride and groom, because they have been reflecting on their own about the meaning and importance of this event. Instead, I want to speak to the rest of us, because I think we all bring marriages with us into this place. We bring our parents' and grandparents' marriages. We are the living products of their unions. What we have learned in life about love and anger and closeness and fairness and sexuality we have learned in large measure from them. So we carry our parents' and grandparents' marriages around in our bodies and our minds. They are with us today.
>
> Even if we have never been married, we bring a marriage here as well. We bring a marriage of our fantasies. We bring a marriage that we think we might want to have in the future, or maybe have decided not to have. As we look at a new marriage beginning, we think about what we might want out of a marriage, and what we

want to avoid. We say to ourselves, when we observe other couples present here: "I would never act like that if I were married," or "I would never put up with that," or "This is what I would want if I were married." And so we dream of our ideal mate.

If we are divorced or widowed, we bring here today the marriage of our past and possible marriage of our future. We remember our own wedding day, a beginning that we thought would not end, but did. We regret what was bad about the marriage or how it ended, but we try to concentrate on celebrating what was good. If we've been through a divorce, we may be inspired by the hope this wedding represents, hope that enduring, loving unions are indeed possible in a fragile world.

If we come as married people, particularly if we are happily married, we renew our marriage here today. We remember our decision to marry, and whether it was a tortuous decision or an easy one. We remember our wedding day, how we felt, how our lover looked, who was with us then and is still with us, and who has passed from our lives. We remember the little things that went wrong, as when I said "With this wing, I thee wed." We remember the enthusiasm we began our marriage with, our vast hope for the future, our certain sense of being a special couple unlike any other. We remember that day as the beginning of the exquisite and perilous adventure our marriage has been.

My message to you today is that this wedding only appears to be just for Bill and Colleen. It is really Bill and Colleen's gift to us.

INTENTIONAL WEDDINGS

Like many other couples in the early 1970s, David and Jill dispensed with the traditional wedding ritual in favor of a ceremony in a meadow outside of town. Jill wore a peasant dress and flowers in her hair, and David wore new jeans and sandals. They included readings from the mystic Kahlil Gibran and the psychotherapist Fritz Perls. The minister was from the local university student center. As a guest, I thought it was a refreshing break from stale traditions. But I also remember the apologetic parents, the bewildered extended family members, and the constant concern that the sky would produce a downpour. The family had no part in the planning, and no role in the ceremony itself. The wedding was intentional all right, but it was an ultimate expression of 1960s generation-gap individualism.

Some couples do in fact plan their weddings as rebellions against their families, but most, despite unprecedented freedom to do their own thing, choose a wedding celebration that is pleasing to family and friends, and that has some of the traditional elements. But, once you opt for traditionality, being intentional about a wedding ritual becomes more complicated, because tradition carries so much baggage for so many people. (Second marriages are easier, because there are fewer cultural expectations. See Chapter 11.) The following suggestions are intended for those couples who want certain elements of the traditional wedding, but who also want to be intentional about the planning process and the ritual itself.

- *Be clear about your core values and wishes.* You might be firm in your decision, for example, that only you will choose the type of religious ceremony, even though your spouse's faith is different from your family's. If your parents are divorced, you might insist, despite your mother's wishes, that your father be invited to the wedding and escort you down the aisle. If you are financially independent and intend to pay for most of your wedding, let your parents know this from the outset. The key is to have a basic list of irrefutable values and priorities guiding your wedding.
- *Be willing to compromise on everything else.* Couples with too long a list from the preceding may find themselves constantly squabbling with their families. They have forgotten or haven't yet realized that a traditional wedding is for everyone. An example is Mary Alice, a 26-year-old who insisted that her mother's sister Louise, whom Mary Alice thought crude and offensive, be excluded from the guest list, even though all the other aunts and uncles were invited. Mary Alice's mother, of course, would not hear of such a breach of etiquette, whereupon a month-

long battle ensued before Mary Alice surrendered. Compromise, of course, does not always mean acquiescing. Although Mary Alice did agree that Father Richard, her mother's brother, officiate at the wedding, she compromised by having her favorite local priest co-officiate with him.

• *Find ways to express your own values, while not excluding those of your family, your community, and your religious and ethnic traditions.* Patrick and Lea Anne had a Catholic wedding that began with the very traditional Catholic hymn "Holy God We Praise Thy Name." Other music included a bagpipe piece that represented Patrick's fondness for Scotland, and a song he composed and sang to his bride during the ceremony. The priest officiated in traditional ritual vestments and conducted the full service of the Eucharist, but Lea Anne and Patrick memorized their vows and recited them without the priest leading them through phrase by phrase. In other words, there were both traditional wedding elements so that the families felt comfortable that this was the "real thing," along with personal touches to make the wedding an intentional reflection of the couple. There is wisdom in the old expression, "something old, something new . . ."

• *Be a good sport.* Once you agree to a traditional wedding, it will probably be impossible to avoid the standard wedding reception antics such as throwing the bridal bouquet and garter. Patrick and Lea Anne went through these rituals quickly and with humor, and their single friends played along gamely. They even went along with the required kiss after guests clinked their glasses in unison—but just the first two times. The third time, they arranged for the groom to kiss the matron of honor and the bride to kiss the best man. The audience was taken aback, then, having tweaked the traditional ritual in this way, the couple proceeded to kiss with good humor throughout the rest of the evening whenever glasses tinkled.

• *Involve the groom in the planning and preparation.* The tradition of the bride-to-be (along with assorted other female assistants) doing most of the wedding planning sets an unfortunate precedent for marital partnership. The groom should take responsibility for certain tasks; for example, he could check out reception facilities and photographers, handle the legal paperwork, or manage the logistics with the religious institution. He might have interests and abilities in other areas as well, including those more traditionally assigned to women, such as invitations, menus, and flowers. If family rituals are enhanced by maximum participation, the wedding planning benefits from active involvement by both bride and groom. However, since this kind of participation from the groom is unorthodox, the bride might have to run interference with her mother, who might think the groom is stepping out of line or that his mother is exerting too much influence. The groom, for his part, will have to learn early to negotiate with his future mother-in-law if she is active in the planning. But remember, serious disagreements are best worked out between blood relatives.

Weddings don't just signify a major life passage: They make it happen. In every culture throughout human history, communities have ritualized the change from the single state to the responsibilities and privileges of the married state. For families, weddings are the most memorable of all family rituals, resulting in innumerable photos and stories. They represent the end of one phase of the family life cycle and the beginning of a new one. They offer the promise of marital happiness and children, while carrying the concern that it may not work out. Weddings are a huge expense, an enormous amount of work to put on, and it may take months for the principals to recover. Weddings lift the couple and their families onto center stage, in the bright lights of their community, in the universal human drama of new love.

FUNERALS

A funeral is not a ritual for the dead, it is for the living who need to mark the passage from life to death and to gather for support in a time of loss and sadness. Cultures differ drastically in the specifics of funeral ceremonies, but they all enact rituals of death and mourning.

In contemporary America society, a funeral is often a significant event during which elderly family members and old friends
come together. They are past the life stage when their children
are getting married, and they spend holidays and other internal
family rituals with their closest kin. Perhaps they only see their
oldest friends, cousins, and even siblings infrequently. But a
death galvanizes the whole social network. My parents used to
say that you know you are old when the obituaries are the first
place you look in the newspaper. Far from morbid, this interest
in the dead represents loyalty to one's social convoy, the people
with whom you have traveled for a lifetime.

Family deaths, of course, are not discovered in the newspaper
and they propel the family into a torrent of emotion and flurry of
immediate and difficult decisions. Funeral rituals are as complex as wedding rituals, and as public, but there is far less time
to weigh options and accommodate the family's values and beliefs. Although there are many ethnic, religious, and individual
family variations, funerals in the United States commonly involve at least four types of social ritual: the wake or visitation,
the funeral service, the burial, and the reception.

Being intentional about death ceremonies is challenging in a
society that has "professionalized" the death experience. Until
well into the twentieth century, most people died at home while
in the care of their families. Families generally knew their loved
one was failing, and thus could begin to attend to the details of
funeral and burial arrangements. The casket was purchased
from a local furniture maker, the religious services were scheduled, and the body was buried in a plot on the family land or in
the local cemetery. Embalming was not done because there was
no need for a wake or viewing (the body was in view on the
death bed) and the burial was accomplished in a timely fashion.
It was only during the Civil War that preserving bodies through
embalming began in the United States, because families wanted
the bodies of their dead shipped home for burial.[4]

In the late nineteenth century, although family members often were still present at the death, funeral directors (a then new
profession) took over the process of preparing the body for the

funeral, generally in the home. Many of the first funeral directors were also furniture and casket makers who gradually added the functions of embalming and burial to their business. What were termed Protestant, Catholic, Jewish, and Black funeral homes sprung up around the country, and families developed loyalties to certain funeral directors. In short order, the funeral home evolved into a one-stop shopping service: casket, cemetery, body preparation, a setting for the wake, funeral notices, funeral carriage, and legal paperwork all were taken care of. The funeral profession evolved as a family business, passed on through generations. Even today, about 85 percent of funeral homes are family-owned, and have been for an average of 44 years, although funeral conglomerates are growing rapidly.[5]

The distancing of families from death and death ceremonies was furthered in the twentieth century when the dying process itself was moved to the hospital. For the first time, the family and community were cut off from direct, in-home contact with the dying person. Just as the development of the funeral profession meant families didn't have to deal with the aftermath of death, the medicalization of death also meant they weren't prepared for it. The result now is widespread discomfort with both death and death ceremonies, and a reliance on professionals whose recommendations may be influenced by their professional training and often their financial interests rather than the needs of the bereaved.[6]

Gregory Young, a former funeral director, summarized the changes in the American way of death in this way:

> Once funerals [came to be] conducted outside of the home, death was no longer regarded as a normal part of life. An aging or sick relative was not as likely to die at home now that there were hospitals and nursing homes. Unlike years past, children did not witness the illness and death of aged relatives. Instead, the phone would ring and the survivors would learn of the death. The funeral home would then be called, and later the family would arrive to make the necessary arrangements. The body was not seen until visiting hours a day or two after death. . . . In some cases, the

body was not viewed. Families did not care to ask about the process by which the body was prepared, since the procedure was no longer performed in the home. They arrived at the funeral home at a determined hour and walked into a room where the body had been placed in its casket, flowers appropriately positioned, and chairs provided for friends. Family members would continue, and often add to, the services their ancestors had handed down, but they became isolated from the process. The funeral director handled everything, as their agent and buffer. The family only saw the end result. They were asked what services and goods they wanted to select from the "menu," and when they returned, it had been done. I have always argued that funeral directors provide a valuable service by taking on all the complicated and time-consuming details for a bereaved family, thus allowing relatives and friends to mourn as they see fit. But what funeral directors also do in sparing the surviving family members from having to deal with such concerns, is to significantly reduce their involvement in the grieving process. . . . A family ignorant of its alternatives, or too trusting of the funeral director, is ripe for being misled.[7]

THE INTENTIONAL FUNERAL

Like traditional weddings, death rituals are public rites with long traditions and religious underpinnings, and they are mounted for the community as well as the family. But at the time of death, the family is far needier than at the time of a marriage, and far more rattled. Being intentional about death rituals ideally begins well before a death, in the form of discussions among family members about their needs and wishes. This kind of discussion is best held before anyone is terminally ill; that is, before the pain of loss predominates in the family's consciousness. Find answers for such questions as: How do you and your loved ones feel about cremation, about open caskets at wakes, about certain traditional or nontraditional religious ceremonies, about eulogies, about the music, about who should be invited to the ceremonies, about which funeral home and cemetery to use, or where the ashes should be placed? Even once someone is seriously ill, having this kind of discussion can relieve everyone of the burden of wondering what the person *would have* preferred for his or her funeral rituals. It can also give family members the chance to express their own wishes, since, as noted, funeral services are really for the living.

Whose Funeral Is It Anyway?

Being intentional about funerals means more than simply drawing up a list of personal preferences. Ideally, the choices families make should stem from reflection on the deeper needs that death ceremonies can meet. In other words, how can these rituals honor the dead person and help the family and its community? Earnest Morgan described seven needs that death ceremonies can meet when they are thoughtfully planned:[8]

Reestablish Relationships

Funerals can be a time of family reunion and reconciliation. If you have distant relatives, cut off from the family, delaying the wake and funeral for a few days to give them time to arrive is a clear indication to them that you want them with the family at this time of mourning. Similarly, a service open to the whole community of people who knew the deceased, as opposed to a small private service, can serve the purpose of connecting the family with people who have dropped out of the family's orbit but who occupy a special place in the family's history. I remember the joy I felt at seeing our former next-door neighbors at my father's wake; and Jim, my old friend from second grade, who attended the funeral with his own father who would soon pass away. Absent an event announced as open to our whole community, these old friends might not have brought the special supportive memories that only old friends can offer.

Identification with the Deceased

Death ceremonies allow family members and friends to focus on the values and life lessons taught by their loved one. When my friend Cindy Skipper died, a young woman with three small children after a long bout with breast cancer, her husband Peter and their friends created a splendid ritual of celebration of her remarkable life of courage and service to others. Peter spoke powerfully at the service about what her life meant for everyone present. A well-planned service shines an intense spotlight on a unique human life.

Affirmation of Values

A death requires that we think about what is important in our lives. Death rituals can focus our priorities—how we use our time, and how we regard our relationships. I remember a minister saying that he had counseled many dying people over the years, but had never heard one person express regret that he or she had not spent more time on the job.

Relief of Guilt

Surviving family members and friends frequently feel pangs of remorse about their relationships with the deceased and a sense that it is "too late" to make amends. Thoughtfully planned services can give these individuals the sense that they are honoring their loved one and partly making up for the past. Even more powerful is the infusion of love from friends and other family members who support and do not judge past deeds.

Bob had stopped talking to his father after his father would not accept the fact that Bob was gay, or his life partner. When his father died suddenly, Bob immediately decided, despite his feelings of anger, guilt, and fear of rejection, to return home for the funeral. He not only experienced a reconnection with his family, but also came to greater peace with both his own and his father's actions at the time of their estrangement. Sometimes, as when death is the result of suicide, guilt is palpable. It is important to choose someone for the memorial sermon who can speak words of perspective and self-forgiveness for the survivors.

Rehabilitation

When an old person dies who has been deteriorating for many years and bears little resemblance to a once vibrant family member and friend, death ceremonies can be used to redirect the survivors' attention to the person's better years. Earnest Morgan describes the funeral services for his father-in-law, whose mental abilities had declined greatly in his last years. The family decided to not have an open casket, and instead focused the memorial service "on what a fine strong person he had been." The effect left those in attendance with a restored vision of this man whose passing had actually been an occasion for relief.

Religious Observance

Because death stirs up the ultimate human concerns, religious services can offer great comfort and meaning to the survivors. They can also help to unify an entire nation, as after President John Kennedy was killed. Some families participate, perhaps reciting a favorite poem of the deceased, singing a favorite hymn, or having a family member deliver a eulogy. Other families prefer a traditional and familiar service.

I remember the solace at my father's solemn high funeral mass, the mass that I had assisted at as an altar boy so many times as a child. My cousin, Maryknoll priest Jack Halbert, delivered a very personal sermon, describing the ways in which we could achieve a sense of divine revelation through contemplating my father's life—including his virtues and his shortcomings. And at the end of the service, just before that long, hard procession out of the church, the pastor came to the family pew and told us that he used to watch for my father's reactions every Sunday during the sermon. When my father nodded, the pastor figured he was getting it right. This remark mixed laughter with our tears, and gave us strength to walk down the aisle and go on to the burial service. Religious services at their best bring together the sacred and the human elements of life and death.

Emotional Support

This is at the heart of death ceremonies. Well-planned rituals offer the family frequent opportunities to give and receive emotional support. At my father's wake, when dozens of family and friends poured in, I remember having an almost physical sense of emotional support coursing through my body, as if from an intravenous infusion. This infusion of support actually begins before the death ceremonies when loved ones start their rituals of visiting, feeding, listening, and helping. Each new wave of tears brought on as I embraced another loved one was not just about grief; there were also joyful tears of being loved and supported at a time of such raw emotional need. A post-funeral meal at the house or catered at a reception center can continue the support after the burial and give guests the chance to plan when they will next check in with the grieving family members.

An intentional funeral, one that reflects the values of the deceased and the family, is most likely to emerge from an Intentional Family that also ritualizes the process of living. If a family is accustomed to asking itself, "What do we want and need here," it is natural to ask those questions when death occurs. But because death may come with no warning, it is best to think and talk along the way about this culminating life ritual. These discussions are likely to be tinged with sadness, but also can be uplifting.

A sorrowful loss for one generation becomes warm memories for the next generation through photos and stories. We pass on our family legacies of connection and strength when we ritualize our times of loss with as much intelligence and care as we do our times of joy.

Part IV

BECOMING A

MORE

INTENTIONAL

FAMILY

CHAPTER

ELEVEN

Intentional Single Parents and Remarried Families

FAMILIES HAVE ALWAYS BEEN DIVERSE in form and structure, despite current nostalgia trends about the traditional family that would have us believe otherwise. That includes single-parent and remarried families. The big difference today is that most families now arrive at these family forms through the route of divorce rather than death.[1] Most single-parent families nowadays are actually two separate family units, one with mother and one with father. With remarriage, these families add stepfamilies. If being intentional about rituals can be helpful for all families, it is especially important for the complicated lives of single-parent and remarried families.

Most families lose their bearings for a time after a marital separation. Both parents are generally very distressed. Depending on their ages, the children usually experience some combination of confusion, sadness, anger, and fear. Not surprisingly, family rituals tend to weaken and even disintegrate in the weeks and months after one of the parents moves out. The parent who stays at home (usually the mother) may feel too overwhelmed to do more than provide the basics of child care, and the parent who moves out may struggle with how to establish a routine life style and a way to be involved with the children. Absent its normal rituals of connection, celebration, and community, the family is adrift.

The Jarvis Family

The Jarvis family broke up after Maria struggled for years to get her husband Jack to be more involved with her and the children, currently a 9-year-old boy and a 7-year-old girl. A skilled hands-on engineer, emotionally, Jack was fairly blank. When Maria asked him to leave, he was devastated; he hadn't believed she was serious about her complaints.

After a couple of months, Jack began to have the children over to his apartment every other weekend, but he never prepared a meal for them, claiming that he was completely incapable of cooking. His other child care skills were also minimal; he had left childrearing to his homemaker wife during their marriage. When the children returned to their mother's house after a visit with their father, they were wild from the lack of structure they lived in over the weekend.

Maria, for her part, was beside herself with worry about her future. With only a high-school education and no current work skills, she didn't know how to get started with her new life. What's more, her own family had disowned her for breaking up her marriage to such a "nice man." Most of her friends were couples, who were now taking sides. Sadly, as in many divorces, Maria experienced major losses in her social convoy.

Faced with these problems, Maria was just going through the motions of taking care of her children. The first ritual casualty after the breakup was family dinners. In the past, Maria had prepared nice meals, made sure everyone was present for dinner around 6:00 P.M., and orchestrated the conversation so that the children were given the chance to talk about their day. After Jack moved out, dinners were served at no fixed time; Maria essentially became a short-order cook, although she all but stopped eating dinner herself. When they did sit down as a threesome, the television would be on, and Maria would not focus the conversation as she had in the past. Maria did not make a conscious decision to stop the family dinner ritual, but she was no longer intentional about it. Consequently, the forces of entropy were quickly asserting themselves in the family.

The second casualty was the bedtime ritual. Jack had never participated in them, and didn't know what to do other than send his children off to bed. After the divorce by bedtime, Maria was so tired she just wanted to be rid of the children, who were showing their stress by whining constantly and fighting with each other. Because she felt guilty about neglecting a longstanding bedtime ritual, she did sometimes read to the children. But it was an empty ritual because of the struggle over whether to do it, and because the children, once they had her attention, did not want her to stop. Consequently, the children sought negative attention during the day as a replacement for positive attention at night.

In the midst of this awful adjustment period came an important annual family ritual: 9-year-old Rick's birthday. Still befuddled about living alone and taking care of children every other weekend, Jack expected Maria to handle the gifts and birthday party, which he expected to come home for. Maria bought the presents, but did not know how to handle the party, which traditionally had involved extended families on both sides. She was at odds with her own family, and had not spoken to Jack's family since the breakup. As for having Jack over, Maria knew that Rick badly wanted his Dad to be present at the party, and that Jack was not likely to have a separate party for Rick. So she invited Jack. The result was the birthday party from hell. After the cake, candles, and presents, the children clung to their Dad and asked him to stay the night. Jack broke down crying and pleaded with Maria to take him back. When she refused and asked him to leave right away, she felt like the Wicked Witch of western Connecticut. Happy birthday, Rick.

RECASTING FAMILY RITUALS AFTER A DIVORCE

Not all families become as disabled as the Jarvises after a marital separation, but most experience significant disruption of their rituals of connection, celebration, and community. The family script has been thrown away, and new ones must be written. The creation of separate family rituals is a key step toward having two families that can each sustain and nurture children and be happy places for the adults.[2]

The first challenge for single-parent families is to see themselves as real families, not just as pieces of a family. When there has been a loss, either through divorce or death, the remaining family members in the household sometimes have trouble seeing themselves as a complete family, albeit a grieving and hurting one.

Through therapy, Maria Jarvis came to realize that, although she felt she couldn't be married to Jack any more, she and the children still constituted a whole family. In addition to the stress and disorganization she was experiencing, she realized that it had not felt "right" to have family meals in the same way without Jack, or to go to the same pizza restaurant they had gone to as a family. That's why she didn't feel she could say no to Jack's coming home for the birthday party; how could birthdays be celebrated without the original family?

> The first challenge for single-parent families is to see themselves as real families, not just as pieces of a family.

The challenge of feeling like a family is even greater for the nonresidential parent, usually the father. How do you create a sense of family every other weekend and a couple of weeks in the summer? Jack Jarvis didn't bring good parenting and family-making skills with him to his nonresidential parenting, but even if he had, the task would have been daunting.

Whether you are a residential or nonresidential single parent, becoming an Intentional Single-Parent Family requires seeing yourself as a real family and acting like one when you are together. For the residential parent who has the children most of the time, this comes down to three strategies:

- Maintaining continuity with the rituals that were working well before.

- Modifying the rituals that no longer work in their original form.

- Creating new rituals for the new family.

After recovering her equilibrium, Maria Jarvis did resurrect several important rituals of connection with her children. She had breakfast with her children before school and asked them about their upcoming day; she made dinner, and turned the television off; and she gave each child undivided time before sleep. Children crave their traditional family rituals during times of stress and turmoil, and adults usually find them comforting as well, despite the extra work. The meals might have to be simpler, the bedtime stories shorter, the Sunday trips to the zoo less frequent, but continuity with past rituals of connection is crucial after a marital separation.

Ritual Modification

Maria had to modify some family rituals because Jack had filled a role she could not or did not want to play. Almost every week, in good weather, the family had gone on a Sunday picnic, after which Jack would play ball and wrestle with the children. Maria had no desire to become athletic, nor had this ever been her style of relating to the children. So she and the children decided they would have their picnic at a different park that had swings and climbing equipment, on which the children could play on their own, under their mother's appreciative eye. Thus, they continued an important outing ritual but in modified form.

After Maria went back to work, she felt she had too little time to talk with her children. When she got off work, she was continually chauffeuring the children from one activity to another. In this regard, she was a typical single mother. According to Patricia Waller, director of the University of Michigan Transportation Research Institute, "Single moms make the most [car] trips daily of any group, often under great stress and distractions."[3] Maria decided to be more intentional about this driving time with her children. She created a ritual, whereby when she was driving only one of the children she would say, of "You tell me one thing about your day and I'll tell you one thing about mine." They repeated the exchange for as many rounds as they liked. At the end, Maria would return to something her child might have said that needed follow-up attention. Another ritual the family created was one that Jack would not have liked: They went out for fast food once or twice a week. What made this a ritual, and not just a quick meal, was that Maria and the children decided together on which night they would go out, they alternated between only two restaurants rather than arguing about where to go each time, and Maria tried to initiate a family discussion at the table. For the children, it was a treat they weren't permitted before the divorce, and for Maria, it was a night away from the kitchen and a time when she could focus on having a relaxed time with her children after a busy day in her new job.

The same kind of ritual rework is necessary when a parent dies. When the O'Leary's mother died, her husband and four young children saw the family's ritual life collapse almost entirely. The father at first was overwhelmed with grief, and later with having to raise four children, a role he had mainly left to his wife. To be sure, he clothed and fed the children, but there was an absence of family rituals, except for an annual trip to the family cabin with extended family. Sadly, not even the children's birthdays were routinely celebrated each year. Years later, the collapse of the family ritual structure still causes sadness and anger to the adult O'Leary children. Looking back, they also realize that there had been a breakdown of support from their extended family and community, who could have intervened to help their father manage the basics rituals such as birthdays.

In contrast to the O'Learys, my friends the Skippers, whom I mentioned in Chapter 8, pulled together as an Intentional Family after the death of Cindy, Peter's wife and the mother of Cassie, Lonnie, and Petey. In addition to preserving their meal, bedtime, and outings rituals, Peter involved the children more in meal preparation, during which time he would spend time talking with whichever child was helping. Family prayers also become more meaningful, as a time to communicate with and about Cindy. They continued to go on their annual camping trip with their former church in Connecticut, and they added regular visits to the cemetery to connect as a family around their memories of Cindy. When the first Christmas came after Cindy's death, they headed for California to create a new way to ritualize the holidays, rather than stay at home and dwell on their loss.

For post-divorce families, certain rituals of celebration can be occasions for demonstrating that the original family can still pull together. Joe DiAngelo came to his daughter Gina's birthday parties for several years after the separation and divorce. Her birthday party had always been a grand occasion for her and the extended family, since she was the oldest of all the grandchildren and her birthday fell on January 1. Joe and Lu Ann, Joe's ex-wife, decided that he would continue to be present to show family solidarity in support of Gina on her birthday. The event also helped keep Joe connected with his former in-laws, with whom he always got along. This arrangement worked for about five years, until Lu Ann remarried. The first birthday party after the remarriage was uncomfortable for the three adults, and Gina could feel the tension. Joe then decided to end his participation in the extended family birthday party and to have his own birthday party for Gina on another day.

The DiAngelo story exemplifies how flexible post-divorce families must be if they are to be intentional about their rituals. It was helpful and constructive for Joe to appear at his daughter's parties in the early years after the separation, just as it is for some parents to attend school conferences together. This level of participation works when the ex-spouses are genuinely cooperative and can put the child's interests first. Some ex-spouses even come together for Christmas Eve gift-opening the first year after their separation, particularly if the divorce is not yet finalized. But they must be aware of what it means and what it does not mean, and be clear to the children that their being together for a family celebration does not mean that they are getting back together. Over time, however, most families of divorce find that they need to create separate celebration rituals, as their separate families and households form their own boundaries. Nevertheless, reuniting for major occasions such as weddings, graduations, and bar mitzvahs are always important demonstrations of support for children of divorced families.

For the nonresidential parent, it is also crucial to maintain former rituals that still work, to modify others, and to create some. The biggest mistake nonresidential fathers make is to have free-form, unstructured weekends with their children that flit from one distracting activity to another. The father eventually runs out of fun things to do with the children, and the children become bored, worn out, and demanding; needless to say, very little parent-child connection occurs under these circumstances. Creating a family atmosphere means both instituting family rituals and having time to just "hang around" rather than trying to be a camp activity director. Nonresidential parents can develop rituals that become special to them and their children. One father, an avid swimmer, took his children swimming every time they visited, and coached them on their techniques, a form of recreation and attention that became special to Dad and his kids.

Thanksgiving, Christmas, Passover, and other important family-focused holidays are often treacherous times for single-parent families. Because being alone without one's children at these times can be terribly lonely and depressing, it is not surprising that some ex-spouses compete for their children. But there is no surer way to ruin a ritual for the children than to make them feel they are hurting one of their parents by being with the other.

When both parents are still involved with the children, most Intentional Single-Parent Families develop fixed holiday schedules in order to balance everyone's needs. In the DiAngelo family, the children alternated Thanksgivings and split Christmas Eve and Christmas Day between households, alternating houses each year. It is crucial that the scheduling of major holiday and religious rituals be routinized in single-parent families, and not argued about. This requires that both parents support the arrangement and manage their own sadness and regret without drawing the children into their inner struggle.

Entropy—the loss of energy, connection, and focus—is the wolf at the door of all families, but especially threatens overburdened, full-time single-parent families and part-time nonresidential families. Single parenting is one of the most difficult tasks in contemporary society. But it also offers the opportunity to start family life anew, to be creative about family rituals, and to involve the children in shaping the family's values and its future. Some of the most highly intentional families I know are single-parent families, as are some of the most overwhelmed and entropic. The key differences appear to be the ability of the single parent to focus on what is most important about family rituals of connection and celebration, and on the degree of support from the extended family and community.

REMARRIAGE AND FAMILY RITUALS

As difficult as they can be, single-parent families don't hold a candle to remarried families when it comes to complications with rituals. In single-parent families, there generally is one ritual tradition to draw on from the previous household. In remarried families that follow divorce, there are several sets of ritual traditions to contend with—the original family's plus one or two stepparents'. People approaching a second marriage often don't realize that they are not just uniting as a couple, but are merging at least two family cultures. Remarried families require the highest levels of intentionality of any form of family life in our culture. Otherwise, the forces of entropy will push them apart rapidly.[4]

The preparation for a remarried family begins during the courtship of the couple, when the couple is establishing its own rituals of connection by spending long periods of time alone getting to know and enjoy each other. They must decide on the timing of involving the new partner with the family's rituals. If the children feel that the new romantic partner in Mom's or Dad's life is brought into core family rituals—such as Christmas and birthdays—too soon, before there is a clearly committed relationship, they might reject that person at the outset. Such intimate participation in the family's ritual life should probably be postponed until the relationship is serious and there has already been a good deal of bonding with the children.

Planning for the remarriage itself is pivotal in the formation of a remarried family. Family therapist Janine Roberts describes how she and her future husband decided to have a year-long engagement in order to emotionally prepare everyone, including themselves, their children, their parents, their siblings, and even their ex-spouses, for the coming marriage.[5] The good news is that because remarriage rituals are not as culturally scripted as first marriages, there is a lot of room for intentionality. The bad news is that the stakes in the wedding planning are very high, because some of the participants are likely to have mixed feelings about the relationship. Children in particular may see the remarriage of one of their parents as the end to the hope that their parents will get back together. Extended family members and friends also have mixed feelings about the breakup of the first marriage, about who was responsible, and about the likely success of the second one. Even though (usually) not invited, ex-spouses are a felt presence at the remarriage ceremony. The ghost of marriage past hovers over the ceremony.

The Second Time Around

It is tempting for remarrying couples to want a quick, simple ceremony and to avoid the intricate planning of a more elaborate wedding ceremony. Family therapists who study rituals generally see this as a mistake, because it may not give the children, extended family, and friends the opportunity to deal with their feelings about the new marriage and to offer their support. A more connecting approach involves the children, both young and adult, in the remarriage ceremony, as a step to help solidify the new family. Some couples even have their children come in with them, recite words of support for the new marriage, and leave as a new family. These kinds of rituals can speed the process of forming an integrated new family. The same is true for extended family and friends: participating in the wedding ritual gives them the chance to emotionally accept the new couple and family into their social convoy.[6]

Daily rituals and rituals of celebration can be tricky in the early years of remarried families, especially if there are children from both sides. George Johnson brought into the remarriage a quiet 7-year-old daughter who lived with him part-time. Their dinnertime ritual had been a low key father-daughter conversation, often with long periods of silence since neither was very talkative. In contrast, Geri Stephens had two in-your-face teenagers and a more random dinner ritual that involved loud talking, arguments, and a television blaring in the background. In the midst of an argument over dinner rituals, George used the term "barbarians" to describe her children, which Geri never let him forget. She countered with an attack on his daughter's "lack of personality," a criticism he never let her forget. Each felt accused of being a poor parent. The truth was, they were both good parents but had to learn to blend the cultures of their family rituals. In therapy, they learned to compromise and create daily rituals they all could live with. In the case of dinner, the television was turned off but there was no censoring of the level and tone of the conversation, although Geri did agree to avoid bringing up disciplinary matters during the meal.

Are You Talking to Me?

Children in remarried households sometimes use family rituals to show their negative feelings. Geri's teenage daughter Carrie would not talk to her new stepfather at dinner. After months of being ignored and feeling hurt, George told Geri he would not eat with the family anymore. This precipitated the crisis that sent them into therapy. Geri felt helpless to make her daughter relate to her new husband, and she did not want either her daughter or her husband to boycott family dinners. In family therapy, the couple realized that their meal ritual was being influenced by Carrie's silence toward George. Geri would focus on Carrie in order to draw her in the family conversation, thereby making George feel like even more of an outsider. Their solution was twofold: George would work on not regarding Carrie's behavior as a personal insult; he realized he was a convenient target for Carrie's displeasure about the marriage, coupled with her typical teenage woes. Geri would engage George in the conversational loop and resist the temptation to pursue Carrie to get involved. Eventually, time, patience, and Carrie's growing maturity elevated family dinner rituals from awful into the acceptable range. Remarried family rituals, especially in the early years, may not be highly satisfying, but to discard them is to undermine the formation of the new family.

Stepparent-Stepchild Rituals

Stepparents can use rituals of celebration to forge bonds with their stepchildren. Birthdays in particular offer opportunities for the stepparent to offer the child a personal gift, not one given in conjunction with the biological parent. George found that giving sporting equipment to Geri's teenage son Curt on his birthday gave them something to share during the rest of the year. In the same way, a stepparent can develop special outing rituals that the children might not have done with either of their original parents. One stepfather, an avid hiker, initiated an annual camping trip ritual with his stepson. The first year, the mother had to renege at the last minute because of a work commitment. Her husband and son went anyway and had a wonderful time. In subsequent years, the trip became something the stepfather did alone with his stepson. Mom wisely stayed away. In another family, the new stepmother bonded with her stepdaughter through the ritual of shopping trips, followed by a stop for ice cream on the way home. These kinds of connecting rituals can slowly build a one-to-one relationship between a stepparent and stepchild.

One for All

In the midst of all these efforts to facilitate bonding between one's new spouse and the children and stepchildren, it is important that parents maintain rituals of connection with their own children. Remarried parents sometimes make the mistake of trying to "blend" the new family by not paying special attention to their own children. Ross White, a 30-year-old man, still had painful memories of what happened between him and his father after his father remarried following the death of Ross's mother. For years, Ross and his father had gone to baseball games together, their core ritual of connection. Ross's new stepmother opposed this outing because she thought that one-to-one time between her husband and his children undermined the unity of the new family. Under this pressure, Ross's father abandoned the ritual. Many years later, Ross still felt abandoned by his father. The most successful remarried families encourage special rituals of connection between parents and their biological children, without seeing these as separative.

Family vacations are often the stuff of nostalgia: the family cabin, the beach, the trip to the mountains, the visits with grandma in the country, and so on. Figuring out what to do with two different family vacation traditions requires high levels of diplomacy and skill. Intentional Remarried Families tend to discuss and negotiate vacation plans far in advance, rather than wait until decisions *have* to be made. Sometimes the logistics of a complete family vacation in this circumstance are nearly impossible to negotiate, especially if the children spend considerable vacation time with their nonresident parent. There can be four adult vacation schedules to juggle, plus the children's activities. Even if the family can find a time to vacation together, not everyone will be pleased with the plan, and to accommodate such dissension, smart remarried families alternate trips to give each side of the family the chance to do what they previously enjoyed doing. Letting everyone know that turns will be taken can cut down on the complaining and resistance. Other families deliberately plan activities neither had done previously. Overall, it is best not to force family vacation rituals in the early years of a remarried family. They are better finessed, experimented with, and nurtured along until the new family finds its groove.

Nowhere do loyalties to old rituals surface more than during the holidays, at least for families who celebrate them. Thanksgiving and Christmas are defined by convictions of how the rituals should be done "correctly" in all details. Children tend to be conservative when it comes to holiday rituals; they like things the way they have been. Therefore, the most successful remarried families form a creative amalgam of holiday rituals. They use existing rituals from both sides of the family, and they institute their own new rituals. This delicate process is best conducted through open discussion rather than decreed by the parents. Each suggestion should be treated with respect in the conversation; parents may have to enforce this rule because children may ridicule the ideas of the stepparent or stepsiblings. Holidays are best approached experimentally in the early years of remarried families, assuming that some rituals will work and in the new family dynamic others will not. Settling into an accepted pattern of holiday rituals may take five years or more, even for highly intentional remarried families.

RITUALS OF PASSAGE IN REMARRIED FAMILIES

Major transition rituals such as graduations, weddings, and bar mitzvahs often prove to be a litmus test for remarried families. This section describes one family's bar and bat mitzvah experiences as examples.

The bar mitzvah experience is a ceremonial rite of passage that marks a Jewish male's 13th birthday and his assumption of adult religious responsibilities in the Jewish community. And since the 1950s, the bat mitzvah has initiated female children in the same way. This centuries-old tradition plays a significant role in contemporary Jewish family life.[7]

As for weddings, the ritual of the bar mitzvah begins long before the actual event and has an effect long after. The advance planning is extensive, including the guest lists, invitations, seating arrangements, and menu decisions, all of which include the participation of the extended family and community. Naturally, these negotiations can cause much tension in families, but they can also be used to begin the process of positive transformation from one era of the family's life to another.

Although the 13-year-old boy or girl is the individual in the spotlight in this ritual, reenacting a highly charged drama that demonstrates Hebrew language skills, knowledge of the Torah, and public speaking, the family too is "on stage." The child's performance is a measure of how successful the family has been in preparing the child for this moment and his or her future. And the ceremony itself is a demonstration of the family's ability to enact public rituals.

In divorced and remarried families, the bar or bat mitzvah is a public display of how united the family can be in supporting its growing children. Do both parents show up? How do they act toward each other? How do the stepparents behave? How much tension are the children under? The divorce and its aftermath may loom larger than the ceremony itself. On the other hand, these rituals can help resolve the hurt and ongoing tensions of the divorce experience. Estrangements between family members can be healed and lines of responsibility reshuffled. Rituals of passage such as bar and bat mitzvahs can be much more than ceremonies; when planned and carried out by Intentional Remarried Families, they have the power to transform.

Following is the story of how one remarried family dealt with the bar and bat mitzvah rituals for its four children. Following a protracted period of tension and struggle, including a custody battle, in 1969, Sylvia Kaplan ended her marriage after 11 years and 4 children. Her ex-husband Ron saw the children regularly on weekend visits, and was an involved nonresidential father; but the tension continued between the ex-spouses. Finally, though, after both Sylvia and Ron remarried, things settled down. The first bar mitzvah, which occurred before either parent was remarried, was the first time Sylvia and Ron and their extended families had to deal with each other in a public way following the divorce.

Each of the four children had a very different experience with the bar/bat mitzvah, and each served as a special resource in redefining and renewing the family. Of course, not every remarried family will be able to achieve this level of reconciliation, but the experience of Sylvia's family can teach us all what is possible in remarried families when all the adults rally for the children. Sylvia Kaplan, my colleague and friend, tells the story here in her own words.

Michael's Bar Mitzvah, 1972

Michael is the oldest, and therefore his bar mitzvah, representing the first fledging efforts at a genuine reconciliation, was the first to occur. In many ways, his was the most unorthodox and required the greatest suspension of disbelief. Yet it worked, and was an extraordinary and transformative experience for all of us. Michael was almost 13 and had not gone to Hebrew school, a prerequisite for the bar mitzvah ritual. (He perhaps suffered the greatest fallout from my commitment to progressive and liberated childrearing which is no doubt why he lives an orthodox, structured religious life today.) I had fully supported his earlier decision to quit Hebrew classes when he found them not to his liking. It was only when my sister and I saw a film with a moving bar mitzvah scene that we were jointly motivated by the profoundest sense of longing and regret to seek a bar mitzvah for our sons. Michael and his cousin Jaime were not adequately prepared, but as it turned out, it wasn't necessary. I belonged to a reform temple at the time and they were willing (for a variety of reasons) to accommodate some congregants with special needs. The rabbi was pleased to arrange a joint bar mitzvah for Michael and his cousin in just six months. They would learn the prayers phonetically with the use of cassette tapes. Every-thing would be arranged. This all happened two years after the divorce and before either Ron or I were remarried.

I made all of the plans for the ceremony and the party after-ward. I did this unilaterally, although Michael's father submitted his own guest list. I do not remember who paid or how that was decided, so clearly, money, which is often the stressor in joint celebrations after a divorce, was not a central issue here. This was the first time that my former husband and I appeared to-gether at a public event where we had co-host responsibilities, and it was the first time I would be exposed to much of his ex-tended family and some of our friends who had been extremely critical of my decision to seek the divorce. They were con-vinced the children would be strung out on drugs or showing other signs of abuse or neglect, and seemed pleasantly surprised to see that they were well. My ex-husband and I were both committed to "showing well," as were the children, and the per-formances that day continued well after the ceremony ended. Ron did not appear on stage with Michael as it is traditional for fathers to do. This was ostensibly done out of consideration for our nephew, whose own father had disappeared nine months earlier, a great embarrassment to both sides of that family.

There was certainly a lot for the guests to talk about while they enjoyed their moussaka, but their whisperings did not in-terfere with the good feelings of the day. Michael, the eldest, the one who was most apparently burdened by the divorce experience, scored a personal public triumph that affirmed both his autonomy from the family and his connection to it. Ron and I shared a joint pride in his accomplishment, which allowed me for the first time to feel positive about our contin-ued connection. I felt legitimized as the mother of the bar mitz-vah boy; this was for me an official return to the larger Jewish community. Ron remembered his own bar mitzvah with some nostalgia and felt connected to his oldest son by that expe-rience. So what did it matter if the kid didn't play baseball? His use of humor in his bar mitzvah speech demonstrated that indeed, the apple didn't fall far from the tree.

Rick's Bar Mitzvah, 1974

Rick became a bar mitzvah two years later, shortly before my remarriage. His father had remarried the year before and there were now stepsiblings on both sides. This was the first event where we would all be together. Our fiery foe days were now well behind us. The decision had been made not to fight about child support, and we now had a cordial, although still distant, relationship. Small steps forward were immediately obvious. I shared the wording of the invitation with Rick's father before it was ordered. More significantly, I was pleased to have Ron take his rightful place as father with his son on the pulpit. Rick was the "star" in the family and his stellar performance energized us all. Once again we downplayed our competition with one another because of the joint objective of showing well to our family and friends. The importance of this rite of passage for our family was that, for the first time, the new mates were present and played significant roles. Both Ron's new wife Mary, and my new husband Sam are extraordinarily warm and hospitable people. In a public setting, they made everyone feel welcome and comfortable. The children were relaxed and happy to see the four of us together. Divorce was still relatively uncommon among middle-class Jews in our city and people had no precedent for this kind of thing. My husband Sam and I were very much aware that we were presenting a new model for how divorced couples should deal with one another. We received many compliments from grateful and admiring guests who had attended other such events where the pain and the tension were palpable.

Kerri's Bat Mitzvah, 1977

Kerri's bat mitzvah was again another time and another place. Sam and I were now well married, and the conservative congregation where our family now belonged and where Kerri's ceremony was held was Sam's and not Ron's. A bar/bat mitzvah ceremony is a very different experience in the two denominations. In the reform temple, the Saturday morning event is "staged" and involves only those invited to the "performance." Conservative (and orthodox) congregations treat the bar or bat mitzvah as part of the regular Saturday morning service. Preparation for the ceremony is very much a group activity. Much of the benefit of the experience for participants comes from the training, which is shared with classmates. Close friends and family members of the bar/bat mitzvah are given the honor of reading from the Torah that day and appearing on the pulpit with the child. Both Sam and Ron were honored in that way and both gave toasts before the luncheon that followed the ceremony. Mary and I shared the honor of the candle-lighting ceremony the evening before. There was much goodwill between the four parents, and by this time all of Kerri's grandparents were once again comfortable with one another.

Although Kerri's bat mitzvah was a warm and relaxed experience, the major breakthrough would have to await the next one. Jill's bat mitzvah took place almost three years later and would serve to resolve all lingering animosities and to enlarge our family boundaries to include our two families in an extended family relationship.

Jill's Bat Mitzvah, 1980

Jill, the youngest in the family, had long before taken on the role of protector of family continuity and traditions. She was therefore the one who most directly perceived this particular family ritual event as not just "her day" but as everybody's day. She was fiercely involved in the plans for her bat mitzvah and determined that we all properly perform our designated roles. I should note here that not only had our family relationships evolved over the five years since my remarriage, but the synagogue had evolved too. Mothers as well as fathers now shared the pulpit with their sons and daughters. It is common for parents to make a short speech and present the bar/bat mitzvah child with a small symbolic gift. Jill was the first bat mitzvah in the congregation to have four parents with her on the bima. She felt she deserved a crowd, and we were again pleased to be public groundbreakers.

This time we had a big celebration afterward—an evening party, a gala occasion with dinner, a band, and dancing, something we had said we would never do because a nice luncheon was enough for respectable folks. But perhaps because music, dancing, drinking, and merrymaking, in the context of a ceremonial event, can contribute to the transforming power of the ritual, the two families broke through other boundaries. At these times, people often find the courage to do what they would not otherwise do. Humor, as another component of ritual, helps too. Sam and Ron, both of whom enjoy a public forum, found that their jokes worked well together when they shared the podium to welcome everyone to the festivities that night. Ron's ability to joke about his losses in a way that completely "broke up" his audience helped resolve some of the contradictory feelings present in the room. Losses and gains were both acknowledged. Ron's family often uses humor to cover over pain and as a veiled form of hostility. But on this occasion, the humor was about playing through pain and getting on with life; warmth was more apparent than hostility. Maybe I was the one who had "won" in some areas in life, but on the arena of the comedy stage, his triumph was clear.

The real meaning of Jill's bat mitzvah ritual events only came clear during a more private family ritual celebration several days later. The bat mitzvah came only a few days before the Passover holiday and many of the out-of-town family members stayed for the seder. Sam and I had invited to our home not only my family and his, but also Ron and his wife and brothers and sisters with whom I had shared seders so many years before. The good feeling of the bat mitzvah celebration was still very much in evidence and contributed to the success of this "homecoming" experience. We found that we had translated our public performance of "showing well" to a more intimate family setting where the good feelings continued.

The purpose of the Passover festive meal is for the adults to tell their children the story of the exodus of their ancestors from Egypt, so that they will know that they too had been slaves under Pharaoh and had been liberated from oppression. The enormous goodwill of that Passover meal, and the many more that would follow, have been liberating for me, but more so for my children. We have since shared all of our seders (one year, none of the children were here, but the four of us parents were still together), and traveled around the world together to our children's graduations and weddings. The absence of tension, hostility and competition, and the continuing goodwill in this extended family system, have benefited us all. My children remember the days of "oppression" and are grateful to be liberated through the transforming power of family and community rituals.

Remarried families are one of the most complex groups any of us can belong to. In the background is always a loss, either a divorce or a death. In the foreground is always the potential for conflicting loyalties. Using old and new rituals to forge a future of healing and connection is the hallmark of the Intentional Remarried Family.

CHAPTER

TWELVE

Becoming a More Intentional Family

THIS BOOK BEGAN WITH A BAD NEWS/GOOD NEWS scenario. The bad news was that families at the turn of the twenty-first century no longer have a user's manual to guide them on how to live family life. The good news was that this uncertainty opens the path for Intentional Families. In the intervening chapters, I have described how families can use rituals to foster their sense of connection, meaning, and community in a world that pulls families toward entropy. In contemporary family life, love gets you the first tank of gas; being intentional gives you the refills needed for the long journey.

This chapter offers specific strategies for working with your rituals in order to become a more Intentional Family. The first step is to assess your family's current rituals and target some rituals for change. The second step is to develop a strategy for initiating the change. The third step is to evaluate and troubleshoot the changes you have made.

EVALUATING YOUR FAMILY RITUALS

You can start with this question: Are your current rituals meeting your family's needs for connection, meaning, and community? As you consider the various kinds of family rituals discussed in this book—from everyday rituals of connection to special occasions and holidays to public family rituals—which areas do you feel your family ritualizes well and which areas need ritual enhancement? Most families have rituals they are happy with, some they have let slip a bit, others they feel bad about or hate, and still others they wish they could initiate. The following questionnaire might help you in this self-assessment.

Directions

Put a plus sign (+) in the left column if you think this ritual is already strong in your family and does not need much improvement.

Put a zero (0) if you think this ritual could use some improvement.

Put a minus (–) if you think this ritual could use a lot of improvement.

Write "no" if this ritual is not important or you don't want to work on it.

Connection and Love Rituals

_____ 1. We have meals together regularly.

_____ 2. Our mealtimes are full of good feeling and good conversation.

_____ 3. We often share enjoyable family activities at home.

_____ 4. We often share enjoyable family activities away from home.

_____ 5. We have rich holiday rituals.

_____ 6. We share enjoyable family vacations.

_____ 7. We engage in regular positive contact with our relatives.

_____ 8. We celebrate birthdays well.

_____ 9. We have satisfying ways to acknowledge Mother's Day.

_____ 10. We have satisfying ways to acknowledge Father's Day.

_____ 11. (For families with young children) We have satisfying bedtime rituals.

_____ 12. (For couples) We regularly find time alone to talk.

_____ 13. (For couples) We use bedtime as a way to connect at the end of the day.

_____ 14. (For couples) We go out alone together on a regular basis.

_____ 15. (For couples) We celebrate anniversaries in a way that is meaningful to both of us.

Community Rituals

_____ 1. We regularly see family friends.

_____ 2. We are actively involved in a church/synagogue/mosque, or a similar community concerned with beliefs, ethics, and values.

_____ 3. We are involved in neighborhood activities.

_____ 4. We participate in recreational or educational groups and activities (for example, athletic programs, book clubs, support groups).

_____ 5. We are involved in activities to better our community.

_____ 6. (For parents) We talk to our children about social and community concerns.

_____ 7. (For parents) We are active in our children's school.

After answering the questions, look over your responses to examine your strengths and weaknesses in family rituals. Do you see any patterns? For example, does your family enact big occasional rituals better than daily rituals—or vice verse? Are your parent-child rituals stronger than your couple rituals? (This is often the case in families with young children.) How do your community rituals compare to your internal family rituals? After identifying family ritual areas that you want to improve, ask yourself the follow-up questions about each of them:

1. *Is a ritual missing where you would like one to be?* Are there areas that you don't ritualize at all but wish you did? If so, do you want to try to create one; for example, a daily couple ritual

of connection? Do you think there is support in your family for creating a new ritual?

2. *What is the current ritual lacking?* Has it become just a family routine? Is it too rigid, such as a holiday meal that must always be taken at the same overwhelmed relative's house? Has it lost meaning, as a prayer before meals that is spoken in rote fashion, or a family reunion that has lost the feeling of connection? Is it too infrequent, such as a couple whose "dates" seldom get planned? Is there disagreement about the ritual or conflict during it, as in arguments over dinner behavior or at children's bedtime? Has it become boring for some family members, such as traditional family trips that teenagers no longer enjoy?[1]

3. *Is there too much responsibility placed on one family member?* Most families have a main ritualizer, often a woman, who ends up bearing too much of responsibility for family rituals. A particular ritual may falter when that person tires of the leadership, as in the parent who gives up trying to get family members to have dinner together instead of grazing on their own, or the spouse who resents being the only one who initiates couple outings. Similarly, Christmas rituals might falter because the Christmas Coordinator grows weary or resentful over carrying the burden alone.

4. *Are family members achieving a balance between individual time and family time?* As my colleagues Paul Rosenblatt and Sandra Titus have pointed out, sometimes family connection requires that people feel they have enough time to be apart. This may be true especially for adolescents, but adults, too, need different amounts of joint activities and alone time. Resistance to certain family rituals that require concentrated time together might stem from family members' need to balance aloneness and togetherness. The solution may be to shorten family time together in order to make it easier to connect. For example, consider cutting a Christmas visit to extended family from seven days to four days to avoid overdosing on family togetherness.[2]

5. *Is an underlying family problem hurting the ritual?* If spouses have serious problems or conflicts, the family's rituals might be the casualty. Family dinners might become infrequent or the

family might stop going on outings or vacations. Avoiding rituals becomes a way to prevent conflict. Families will keep the television on constantly through dinner, for instance, as an unconscious way to prevent conversation and thus possible conflict.[3] If the poor quality of family rituals stems from deeper problems, then the family may have to address these problems first, perhaps through family therapy, rather than try to overhaul their rituals. On the other hand, even troubled families can often enhance their rituals of connection and community if they take a low-key approach and deliberately avoid conflict during them. Couples can begin going on dates but agree not to discuss their problems during these rituals. Or a couple who is skittish about dates might take up gardening or bicycling together—or some other activity that brings them together but that does not require much intimacy.

After you complete your own ritual assessment, invite other family members to do the same. How do their responses compare with yours? If you have taken the time to read this book, and other family members have not, there is a good chance that your intent for changing family rituals will be stronger than theirs. For that reason, and because family rituals are so complex, exercise care in implementing changes. In other words, it is important to be intentional about becoming a more Intentional Family.

THE DELICATE ART OF CREATING OR CHANGING FAMILY RITUALS

Most of us become used to things the way they have been done in our families, even if not always satisfying; family routines and rituals take on a life of their own. Just try to change the time your family opens Christmas presents, and no doubt you will meet with resistance. Change can be especially difficult if the family's patterns give individual members maximum freedom—people eating "on the fly," making visits to relatives optional for the children, or letting them go to bed whenever they please. For these two reasons—the weight of tradition and the desire to preserve independence—family rituals are difficult to institute or modify.

The most immediate challenge you face when recommending new or different rituals is that your relatives might see you as trying to control the family unilaterally. They know that the person who controls the family's rituals controls the family. The result is that your family may react negatively before they even consider your idea on its merits. For example, if you suggest to your spouse that it might be nice if you both start going to bed at the same time, you are likely to get an elaborate defense of your partner's different sleep needs and a criticism of your own bedtime patterns. "Sure, I could go to bed at 8:00 with you every night, and then lie there and stare at the ceiling fan until midnight while you snore." If you announce to your eat-and-run teenagers that you want to eat together more often, you will likely hear a chorus of indignant remarks about their tight schedules and the poor selection of food you prepare.

> The most immediate challenge you face when recommending new or different rituals is that your relatives might see you as trying to control the family unilaterally.

The worst way to use what you have learned in this book is to charge headlong into trying to unilaterally change your family's rituals. What's a better way? Start with yourself. Clarify the needs you want to meet by a new or modified ritual and the values you want to promote. Needs and values are the best justifications for proposing that the family ship shift its course. These can be your personal needs and values, or your sense of the family's needs and values. For example, the Thanksgiving planner and cook may identify a personal need for more sharing of the workload, in addition to believing that the rest of the family will get more out of the ritual if they participate actively in preparing for it. The best rationale for adding and changing rituals is a combination of "what's in it for me" and "what's in it for others."

Don't introduce the proposed change without a discussion of why such a change might be helpful, or you run the risk of causing an argument. If you just say, "I think we should be having family dinners more often," chances are you will be met with some version of the response, "I can't be home for dinner every night!" In the same way, if you start with a criticism of the current ritual, you are apt to elicit its defense. Don't say, "Nobody helps around here at the holidays," or you will probably hear something like, "I set the table last Thanksgiving when you asked me to."

If there is another adult in your immediate family, I suggest talking to him or her first. If not, check out your strategy with an adult friend or family member. Following are suggested guidelines for you to consider when you talk with family members about changing family rituals.

1. *Choose a peaceful moment for the discussion.* It is generally a mistake to propose changes in family rituals at a moment of tension or conflict. You are apt to come across as angry and demanding. Other family members are likely to either give in with little intention to follow through, or resist being open to your proposal. Wait for a calm time when you all can be constructive.

2. *Explain that you would like to discuss a specific family ritual,* that you have been thinking about this family ritual and want to hear their thoughts as well. Tackle one ritual at a time rather than try to have a global discussion covering all family rituals, unless other family members appear interested in such a general discussion.

3. *Express your feelings or needs related to the ritual.* Examples: "I've been missing what our family dinners used to give us—a feeling of family togetherness"; "Christmas didn't work for me this year because I felt so overwhelmed"; "I miss going to bed with you at night, especially now that that the kids are up so late."

4. *Invite the others to share their own feelings, needs, and thoughts about the ritual.* They may be feeling the same way you do, or very different. You will pick up how much openness they have toward changing the ritual or starting a new one.

5. *Offer your ideas tentatively, rather than definitively*. Once you are ready to make your proposal, keep in mind that family members usually resist feeling pushed into new rituals. Examples of proposals that invite discussion rather than give commands: "Maybe we could figure out a way to have family dinners more often—not every night, but more often than we do"; "I'd like us to talk about how we can share the load more for Christmas next year"; "Would you be willing to talk with me about how we can spend more time together in the evening?"

6. *Negotiate a trial run of a new or modified ritual that balances everyone's needs*. A couple who have no bedtime ritual might agree to try going to bed at the same time, but allow the night owl to get up after the other has fallen asleep—thus balancing the need for contact at night with the reality of independent sleep patterns. The Christmas Coordinator might solicit help in areas that other family members feel interested in sharing, as opposed to doling out assignments and having to enforce them. A single parent with an independent teenage son might negotiate one weekday night that is religiously set aside for a mother-son dinner.

7. *Agree to follow up to determine how everyone likes the new or modified ritual*. People are more willing to try a new ritual if they know they can reject it if it does not work. Even good plans for rituals frequently require adjustments as time goes on.

These recommendations are the *direct route* to creating or changing family rituals: specifying needs, values, and concerns; listening; proposing changes; negotiating before trying something out; and evaluating how it works. A second option is the *indirect route*, which here does not mean manipulative; it means creating an experience before proposing that it become a ritual. The indirect method of initiating or changing rituals has three steps:

1. *Make something happen one time without major comment*. You might say, "Why don't we try something different this time?" If family members go along with it, they may want to continue the new experience. One year I proposed at Christmas that dur-

ing the meal we each express some appreciation to the other family members, as a kind of verbal Christmas gift. I brought it up a few days before Christmas so that everyone could think about what they wanted to say. No one objected. During the meal that year, we had a lovely exchange, a real moment of family intimacy.

2. *Ask how others liked the new activity and if they would like to make it part of the family's ritual in the future.* After our exchange of appreciations, my family decided collectively that we liked it and would add it to our Christmas rituals. There might not have been such ready agreement if I had taken the direct method of proposing a permanent new ritual before we had experienced it once. It's the same with food: It's often best to try prepare a new dish before discussing whether to add it to the family's regular menu. The proof is in the eating—and in the ritual experience.

3. *Negotiate the specifics of the new ritual.* Ideally, everyone should have input into the details of how the new or modified ritual will be incorporated into the family. In the case of my family's new Christmas ritual, we decided to do it just before the family meal rather than during it, because the intensity of the exchange had interfered with the enjoyment of the food.

A third way to initiate or change rituals is to discover that you enjoyed something that has already happened, and propose making it a ritual. As I mentioned earlier, after moving to Minnesota in 1986, my family started going to Davanni's restaurant for pizza with no thought of starting a family ritual. After several months of going every Friday night, we began to realize that we had the makings of a ritual, and decided together to commit to it as such. A temporary routine became a family ritual.

A colleague of mine, a single man without children, took his nephews to a cabin in northern Minnesota one year, then the next, and the next. Before long, he and his nephews realized that it had become a ritual—repeated, coordinated, and significant. Once his nephews reached age 10, they were "eligible" to go with Uncle Art to the cabin. One year when Art proposed going to a different cabin on a different lake, his just-turned 10-year-old nephew objected. "You can't do that," he pleaded. "I've been waiting all my life to go to that cabin with you." Art immediately reasserted the ritual as originally established.

OVERHAULING, SUBSTITUTING, OR DROPPING FAMILY RITUALS

Whatever the method of implementing change—direct, indirect, or through discovery—there needs to be an ongoing process of monitoring the ritual and revising it if necessary. Many once satisfying rituals can lose their meaning as the family or its environment changes. Most rituals need fine-tuning over the years; some need an overhaul, and others need to be substituted or dropped altogether. Major transition times in family life are particularly good opportunities to take a long look at your rituals. For example, after the birth of a first child; after a divorce, a remarriage or a family move; when your last child leaves home; and when your adult children bring new spouses, partners, and inlaws into your family.

After you acknowledge that a family ritual is not working, the key step is to revisit the needs and values that the ritual was intended to serve. What was its original purpose? Are those needs and values still important? In what way is the present ritual not meeting those goals? You may realize that you were expecting a ritual to meet conflicting goals, such as a family vacation designed to connect the immediate family and all your relatives in New England. Perhaps a family bonding vacation should be taken separately from a trip to see relatives. Similarly, a couple's date that includes other couples may serve as a way to build community but not as a way to build couple intimacy. The ritual is expected to do too much.

A ritual can also become burdensome. As my family of origin expanded with siblings and cousins marrying and having children, the number of Christmas presents exchanged grew exponentially. This began to tax everyone's pocketbooks and time constraints. Eventually, a courageous and prudent cousin proposed that we stop exchanging Christmas presents among the cousins and their children. Everyone readily agreed. We were still free, of course, to exchange gifts with a cousin to whom we felt particularly close, but we were no longer expected to come up with presents for the whole clan.

A family ritual may have served its purpose and is best put to rest. My Aunt Nancy and her children always came to my family's house on Christmas Eve for an exchange of presents. It was a wonderful bonding time for the two families. But as everyone grew up, married, had in-laws and then children, this Christmas Eve ritual became difficult to sustain, and so was ended. If my mother and her twin sister had insisted on it, the ritual would have become forced and hollow, with more people each year absenting themselves. We did continue to have a birthday party on December 26 so the two families could be together for the holidays; this event became the substitute for the Christmas Eve ritual. In the same way, bedtime rituals with children serve an important role for many years, but eventually must give way to other forms of connection. And even Christmas Coordinators get old and tired and must share and eventually relinquish their central role in holiday rituals.

PRINCIPLES FOR MANAGING FAMILY RITUALS

Here is a summary of the major principles for successful rituals in Intentional Families:

1. *Adult agreement*. If you and your spouse, partner, or co-parent do not agree on the ritual, it will not work. Take the time to negotiate the needs, values, and goals of family rituals with your adult partner. Otherwise, you alone will be responsible for the ritual's success.

2. *Eventual buy-in from the children*. Older children in particular may resist changes at first, especially if they diminish their freedom and spontaneity. But a ritual that works well will eventually win the allegiance of the children. If they continue to com-

plain and resist, consider overhauling, substituting, or dropping the ritual.

3. *Maximum participation*. The more that family members are involved in planning and carrying out the ritual, the more meaningful it is likely to be.

4. *Clear expectations*. Rituals of all kinds require enough coordination that people know what to do and when to do it.

5. *Minimal conflict*. Although conflict can always pop up in families, the most successful rituals occur without regular tension and conflict.

6. *Protection from erosion*. Entropy threatens all family rituals. Good ritual management means protecting the ritual from the inevitable threats to its consistency and integrity. Good rituals must be fought for.

7. *Openness to change*. Rituals have their seasons for planting, cultivating, pruning, and harvesting. Intentional Families are forever changing while holding onto their important traditions.

BUILDING FAMILY TIES IN OUR MODERN WORLD

The Russian novelist Leo Tolstoy might have been right in 1875 when he wrote in *Anna Karenina* his famous line that "All happy families resemble one another, every unhappy family is unhappy in its own fashion." But Tolstoy was writing in the twilight of the Institutional Family, when families still had a user's manual to follow. In the contemporary Pluralistic Family's montage of family cultures, values, structures, and sexual orientations, each happy family appears to be happy in its own way, but many unhappy families resemble one another because they are pulled apart by the same forces. Perhaps in lieu of a new user's manual, what we need is a more simple guideline. Something like this: Be intentional about your family life, your rituals, and your life in community. When this feels overwhelming, remember, we are all in this together.

Chapter Notes

Chapter 1. The Intentional Family

1. See Steven Mintz and Susan Kellogg, *Domestic Revolutions: A Social History of American Family Life* (New York: The Free Press), 1988, pp. 107–131.

2. For background on changes in family norms from the Psychological Family to the Pluralistic Family in the twentieth century, see William J. Doherty, "Private Lives, Public Values," *Psychology Today*, 25 (May–June, 1990), pp. 32–37, 82; and Judith Stacey, *Brave New Families: Stories of Domestic Upheaval in Late Twentieth-Century America* (New York: Basic Books), 1990.

3. For academic and clinical background on family rituals, see James H.S. Bossard and Eleanor S. Boll, *Ritual in Family Living* (Philadelphia: University of Pennsylvania Press), 1950; Evan Imber-Black, Janine Roberts, and Richard Whiting (eds.), *Rituals in Families and Family Therapy* (New York: W.W. Norton), 1988; Evan Imber-Black and Janine Roberts, *Rituals for Our Times* (New York: Harper-Collins), 1992; Mara Selvini Palazzoli, Luigi Boscolo, Gianfranco Cecchin, and Giuliana Prata, "Family Rituals: A Powerful Tool in Family Therapy," *Family Process* 16 (1977): pp. 445–454; Steven J. Wolin and Linda A. Bennett, "Family Rituals," *Family Process* 23 (1984): pp. 401–420.

4. This definition is my version of Wolin and Bennett's (1984) definition of a family ritual: "a symbolic form of communication that, owing to the satisfaction that family members experience through its repetition, is acted out in a systematic fashion over time." "Family Rituals," *Family Process*, 23 (1984), p. 401.

5. See Wolin and Bennett, "Family Rituals," *Family Process* 23 (1984), pp. 401–420; Evan Imber-Black, "Ritual Themes in Families and Family Therapy," in Imber-Black, Roberts, and Whiting, pp. 47–83.

6. The popular author Robert Fulghum has written about family and community rituals. However, he also refers to certain individual activities, such as personal morning routines, as rituals. I am using the term ritual in the more traditional social science sense to refer

only to social, not private activities. See Robert Fulghum, *From Beginning to End: The Rituals of Our Lives* (New York: Viking), 1995.

7. See John R. Gillis, "Ritualization of Middle-Class Family Life in Nineteenth-Century Britain," *International Journal of Politics, Culture, and Society* 3 (1989): pp. 213–235; John Gillis, "Making Time for Family: The Invention of Family Time(s) and the Reinvention of Family History," *Journal of Family History* 21 (1996): pp. 4–21; Penne L. Restad, *Christmas in America: A History* (New York: Oxford University Press), 1995.

8. For data on parents' spending less time with children, see Joseph Pleck, "Paternal Involvement: Levels, Sources, and Consequences," in Michael E. Lamb (ed.), *The Role of the Father in Child Development*. Third edition. (Hillsdale, New Jersey: Erlbaum), 1996; for documentation of the amount of time spent working, see Juliet B. Schor, *The Overworked American* (New York: Basic Books), 1991.

9. George Gallup Jr. and Frank Newport, "Gallup Survey Finds More Viewers Are Getting Pickier," *Minneapolis-St. Paul Star Tribune*, October 7, 1990, pp. 1F, 7F.

Chapter 2. Family Meals

1. According to a telephone poll of 1,815 randomly selected people in August–September 1995, conducted by RGA Communications Research, Chicago, IL. Final Report, July 1996.

2. See Cecily A. Dreyer and Albert A. Dreyer, "Family Dinnertime as a Unique Behavioral Habitat," *Family Process* 12 (1973): pp. 291–301; and Samuel Vuchinich, "Starting and Stopping Spontaneous Family Conflicts," *Journal of Marriage and the Family* 49 (1987): pp. 591–601. For an interview study showing how dinner conflicts can lead to the avoidance of family meals altogether, see Nancy M. Schwartz, *Family Dinnertime Dynamics: Conflict and Conflict Settlement*, Unpublished Master's thesis (Minneapolis, MN: University of Minnesota), 1988.

3. The classic formulation of ritual phases was given by Arnold van Gennep, *The Rites of Passage* (Chicago: University of Chicago Press), 1960, originally published in 1908. For an adaptation of Gennep's work to family rituals, see David J. Cheal, "Relationships in Time: Ritual, Social Structure, and the Life Course," *Studies in Symbolic Interaction* 9 (1988): pp. 83–109.

4. For figures on carry-out food, see RGA Communications Poll, 1996.

Chapter 3. Rising and Retiring, Coming and Going

1. See Eviator Zeruvavel, *Hidden Rhythms: Schedules and Calendars in Social Life* (Berkeley: University of California Press), 1985. Zeruvavel has done fascinating studies of the impact of time regulation on social life. The daily schedule, for example, did not enter the scene until the medieval Benedictine monks invented the mechanical clock in order to create regularity and punctuality into their daily prayer rituals.
2. *Ibid.*
3. Gallup Organization poll of 1,241 Americans, conducted in August 1990. Reported in *Minneapolis Star-Tribune*, October 7, 1990, pp. 1F, 7F.

Chapter 4. Going Out and Going Away

1. Geoff Sundstrom, *DesMoines Register*, May 27, 1990, p. 4B.
2. C.L. Grossman, *USA Today*, July 5, 1996, p. 5D.
3. For an insightful discussion of the dynamics of family vacations, see Paul C. Rosenblatt and Martha G. Russell, "The Social Psychology of Potential Problems in Family Vacation Travel," *The Family Coordinator* 24 (1975): pp. 209–215.

Chapter 5. Couple Rituals

1. Most of the discussion in this chapter is relevant to all kinds of couples—married, heterosexual, cohabiting, gay and lesbian—because connection rituals are important in all loving, committed relationships. Struggles for heterosexual couples, however, are clearly related to gender differences between men and women. Gay and lesbian couples have a different set of gender issues to contend with. In gay male couples, sometimes neither partner takes the initiative for love rituals outside of sex, while in lesbian couples there is sometimes disappointment with love rituals because of high expectations for closeness. For a discussion of male-female intimacy issues, see Lillian B. Rubin, *Intimate Strangers: Men and Women Together* (New York: Harper & Row), 1983. For a discussion of intimacy issues for homosexual couples, see Sara Steen and Pepper Schwartz, "Communication, Gender, and Power: Homosexual Couples as a Case Study," in Mary Anne Fitzpatrick and Anita L. Vangelisti (eds.),

Explaining Family Interactions (Thousand Oaks, CA: Sage Publications), 1995, pp. 310–343.

2. See, for example, Carolyn P. Cowan and Philip A. Cowan, *When Partners Become Parents* (New York: Basic Books), 1992.

3. Susan Abel Lieberman, *New Traditions: Redefining Celebrations for Today's Family*. (New York: Noonday Press), 1991, p. 85.

4. Quoted in *USA Today*, February 13, 1987, p. D1. The original source was *Country Crock's Perfect Couple Survey*, a 1987 poll of 1,006 couples.

Chapter 6. Special Person Rituals: Birthdays, Mother's and Father's Day

1. For a history of both Mother's and Father's Day, see Ralph LaRossa, *The Modernization of Fatherhood: A Social and Political History* (Chicago: University of Chicago Press), 1997. For the history of birthdays, see Leonore Davidhoff and Catherine Hall, *Family Fortunes: Men and Women of the English Middle Class, 1780–1830* (London: Hutchinson), 1987.

2. La Rossa, *The Modernization of Fatherhood*, pp. 170–192.

3. For a discussion of women's role as family ritualizers, see Micaela Di Leonardo, "The Female World of Cards and Holidays: Women, Families, and the Work of Kinship," *Signs: The Journal of Women in Culture and Society* 12 (1987): pp. 438–453.

4. See David Popenoe, *Life without Father* (New York: The Free Press), 1996.

5. LaRossa, *The Modernization of Fatherhood*, pp. 170–192.

Chapter 7. Thanksgiving

1. Edwin T. Greninger, "Thanksgiving: An American Holiday," *Social Science* 54 (1979): pp. 3–15; Maymie R. Krythe, *All about American Holidays* (New York: Harper & Row), 1962, pp. 232–244.

2. *Ibid.*, p. 237.

3. See Carolyn R. Shaffer and Kristin Anundsen, *Creating Community Anywhere* (New York: Jeremy P. Tarcher), 1993.

4. See Georgia Dullea's humorous article on the loss of turkey-carving skills among contemporary young men, "Real Men Can Cry, But They Can't Carve Turkey Anymore," *The New York Times*, November 21, 1990, pp. B1, B6.

5. See Steven J. Wolin and Linda A. Bennett, "Family Rituals and the Recurrence of Alcoholism over Generations," *American Journal of Psychiatry* 136 (1979): pp. 589–593.
6. Walter Shapiro, "Why We've Failed to Ruin Thanksgiving," *Time*, November 27, 1989, p. 94.
7. Garrison Keillor, "Pleasant Holiday Requires Only Sitting Down to It," *Star Tribune*, November 26, 1992, pp. 1A, 18A.

Chapter 8. Christmas

1. Penne L. Restad, *Christmas in America: A History* (New York: Oxford University Press), 1995, pp. 3–16, 264.
2. *Ibid.*, pp. 91–122. See also William B. Waits, *The Modern Christmas in America: A Cultural History of Gift Giving* (New York: New York University Press), 1993.
3. John Gillis, "Ritualization of Middle-Class Life in Nineteenth-Century Britain" *International Journal of Politics, Culture, and Society,* 3 (1989): pp. 213–236. See also Carrier, James G., "The Rituals of Christmas Giving." In Daniel Miller (ed.), *Unwrapping Christmas*, (Oxford: Clarendon Press). 1993.
4. Waits, *The Modern Christmas in America*, p. 3. For Christmas' reach into the non-Christian world, see Daniel Miller, "A Theory of Christmas," in Miller (ed.), *Unwrapping Christmas*, pp. 22–26.
5. Theodore Caplow, "Christmas Gifts and Kin Networks," *American Sociological Review* 47 (1982): 383–392. This was a 1978 study of a representative group of families in a midwestern city, who were interviewed at length about all the Christmas gifts they gave and received.
6. Theodore Caplow, "Rule Enforcement without Visible Means: Christmas Gift Giving in Middletown," *American Journal of Sociology* 89 (1984): pp. 1306–1323.
7. Garrison Keillor, *Leaving Home* (New York: Viking), 1987, p. 184.

Chapter 9. Community and Religious Rituals

1. The best overview of Putnam's ideas can be found in Robert D. Putnam, "The Strange Disappearance of Civic America," *The American Prospect*, Winter 1996, pp. 34–48.
2. In an earlier book, I criticized therapists for ignoring or even pathologizing community involvements in their clients, and suggested

ways to encourage community involvement. See William J. Doherty, *Soul Searching: Why Psychotherapy Must Promote Moral Responsibility*. (New York: Basic Books). 1995. Two popular writers on psychology also emphasize the community context of mental health and family survival. See M. Scott Peck, *The Different Drum: Community Making and Peace* (New York: Simon & Schuster), 1987; and Mary Piper, *The Shelter of Each Other: Rebuilding Our Families* (New York: Grosset/Putnam), 1996.

3. Putnam, "The Strange Disappearance of Civic America," pp. 34–35.
4. *Ibid.*, p. 45. See also Putnam's original paper for more details than given in the *American Prospect* condensed version: Robert D. Putnam, "Tuning In, Tuning Out: The Strange Disappearance of Social Capital in America," *Political Science and Politics*, December 1995, pp. 664–683.
5. For an analysis of the contemporary tension between individualism and social commitments, see Robert N. Bellah, Richard Madsen, Ann Swidler, and Steven M. Tipton, *Habits of the Heart: Individualism and Commitment in American Life* (Berkeley, CA: University of California Press), 1985.
6. Putnam, "The Strange Disappearance of Civic America," p. 47.
7. Omni Poll for Barna Research Group, Ltd., quoted in *USA Today*, May 3, 1996, p. 1A.
8. Robert N. Bellah, Richard Madsen, William M. Sullivan, Ann Swidler and Steven M. Tipton, *The Good Society* (New York: Alfred A. Knopf), 1991, pp. 217–218.
9. Omni Poll, 1996.

Chapter 10. Rituals of Passage

1. Arnold van Gennep was the anthropologist who pioneered the study of rites of passage. See *The Rites of Passage* (Chicago: University of Chicago Press), 1960, originally published in 1909.
2. See Diana Leonard Barker, "A Proper Wedding," in Marie Corbin (ed.), *The Couple* (New York: Penguin Books), 1978, pp. 56–77; and Diane Leonard Barker, *Sex and Generation: A Study of Courtship and Wedding* (New York: Tavistock Publications), 1980.
3. *Ibid.*, p. 71.
4. Gregory Young , *The High Cost of Dying* (Buffalo, NY: Prometheus Books), 1994, p. 20–23.
5. *Ibid.*, pp. 22–29.

6. Earnest Morgan, *Dealing Constructively with Death*. (Bayside, NY: Zinn Communications), 1994.
7. Gregory Young, *The High Cost of Dying*, pp. 24–25.
8. Earnest Morgan, *Dealing Constructively with Death*, pp. 78–79.

Chapter 11. Intentional Single Parents and Remarried Families

1. For a history of American family life, see Steven Mintz and Susan Kellogg, *Domestic Revolutions: A Social History of American Family Life*. (New York: Free Press), 1988. For a good discussion of family rituals in single-parent and remarried families, see Imber-Black and Roberts, *Rituals for Our Times*.
2. Constance Ahrons, *The Good Divorce*. (New York: HarperCollins), 1994.
3. Quoted in *The New York Times*, August 10, 1996, p. 21.
4. A good discussion in the professional family therapy literature about rituals in remarried families can be found in Mary F. Whiteside, "Creation of Family Identity through Ritual Performance in Early Remarriage," in Evan Imber-Black, Janine Robert, and Richard Whiting (eds.), *Rituals in Families and Family Therapy* (New York: W.W. Norton), 1988. A more popular discussion of rituals in remarried families can be found in Imber-Black and Roberts, *Rituals for Our Times*.
5. Imber-Black and Roberts, *Rituals for Our Times*, p. 23.
6. Mary F. Whiteside, "Creation of Family Identity through Ritual Performance in Early Remarriage." pp. 289–291.
7. See Edwin H. Friedman, "Systems and Ceremonies: A Family View of the Rites of Passage," in Betty Carter and Monica McGoldrick (ed.), *The Changing Family Life Cycle* (Boston: Allyn and Bacon), 1989. And Judith Ron, "Mazel Tov: The Bar Mitzvah as a Multigenerational Ritual of Change and Continuity," in Evan Imber-Black, Janine Roberts, and Richard Whiting (eds.), *Rituals in Families and Family Therapy*, pp. 177–208.

Chapter 12. Becoming a More Intentional Family

1. Wolin and Bennett offer four categories for assessing how families manage their rituals: flexibly ritualized, underritualized, rigidly ritualized, one-sided rituals, and hollow rituals. See Wolin and Bennett, "Family Rituals," *Family Process* 23 (1984), pp. 401–420.

2. Paul C. Rosenblatt and Sandra L. Titus, "Together and Apart in the Family," *Humanitas* 12 (1976): pp. 367–379.
3. See Paul C. Rosenblatt and Michael R. Cunningham, "Television Watching and Family Tensions," *Journal of Marriage and the Family* 38 (1976): pp. 105–111.

Index